P9-DFN-210

MORE RECIPES FOR TIRED TEACHERS

Well-Seasoned Activities for the ESOL Classroom

Contributed by teachers associated with
Pilgrims Language Courses, Canterbury, England

Edited by Christopher Sion

ADDISON-WESLEY PUBLISHING COMPANY, INC.

Menlo Park, California • Reading, Massachusetts
New York • Don Mills, Ontario • Wokingham, England • Amsterdam • Bonn
Sydney • Singapore • Tokyo • Madrid • San Juan

A Publication of the World Language Division

CHRISTOPHER SION holds university degrees in social science and philosophy and took his first qualification to teach English as a foreign language in 1973. Since then he has taught English to speakers of other languages and conducted teacher training workshops in England, Ireland, Germany, Spain, Austria, Belgium, France, and the Netherlands.

Today Chris lives in the south of the Netherlands just a few miles from the German border. His professional life is very much split between these two countries. He teaches English in the Language Training Department of a multinational company near Düsseldorf two and a half days a week and freelances, mainly in the Netherlands, for the rest of the time. He was associated with Pilgrims Language Courses in Canterbury for a number of years.

Other publications of his include *Recipes for Tired Teachers* and many articles in journals such as *Modern English Teacher, The SEAL Journal,* and *Human Potential Resources.*

"How to tell students what to look for without telling them what to see is the dilemma of teaching."

M. L. J. Abercrombie

This book is dedicated to Mario Rinvolucri as a tribute to his drive towards making education less oppressive.

Editorial and production: Jeanine Ardourel & Associates

Manufacturing: James W. Gibbons

Text design by Bonny Chayes Yousefian

ISBN 0-201-52318-3
ABCDEFGHIJ-ML-99876543210

INTRODUCTION

More Recipes for Tired Teachers is a companion volume to the successful *Recipes for Tired Teachers*. Most of the material contained in this edition was originally published by Pilgrims Language Courses, Canterbury, England, under the title *An English Teacher's Scrapbook*. Both books grew out of the realization that Pilgrims' policy of commissioning whole books from individual teachers tended to neglect those other teachers who each had a few excellent classroom ideas. While these ideas were well worth collecting, there were not sufficient numbers to fill one book per teacher. *Recipes* and *More Recipes* provide an outlet for teachers' favorite exercises and for activities which are so simple that no one had previously considered committing them to paper.

The material presented in *More Recipes for Tired Teachers* is intended primarily for teachers of English as a second language or foreign language. However, teachers of other modern languages will find they can easily adapt almost all the recipes to teach Spanish, French, German, Italian, Japanese, or whatever. A further group of teachers who will find a wealth of practical activities and new ideas to enrich their repertoire includes teachers of English (as a first language) or of communication-skills courses at high school level.

The main body of *More Recipes for Tired Teachers* contains fifty-seven practical activities geared to the ESOL/TEFL classroom. These ideas have been contributed by some forty teachers who come from a wide variety of backgrounds and whose teaching experience has been gleaned all over the world. The ideas range from games to grammar, from smells to the seven deadly sins, from cops and robbers to Chinese proverbs. There is something for everyone, be the student a business person, university student, teacher trainee, child, or teenager.

The contributions in *More Recipes* are divided into six units: Attention and Awareness, A Visual Bias, Auditory Activities, Working with Words, Reading and Writing, and Games and Simulations. In addition, there are two appendices. The first is dedicated to teacher development; the second, to "Mini-Recipes."

Each recipe includes, at the top, the level of difficulty, suggested time, the language function(s) developed, practiced, or reinforced, and the materials required. A section called "Before Class" describes preparations that must be made before the recipe is used. (This section is omitted if no specific preparation is required, other than familiarizing oneself with the activity.) The section called "In Class" presents, step by step, the procedure for using the recipe with students. The recipes are clear, concise, and comprehensive. The emphasis in the editing has been on writing explicit instructions. At the same time, it has been assumed that these instructions will be read and interpreted with a fair measure of common sense.

The eight contributions included in the Teacher Development appendix provide teachers and teacher trainees with a range of ideas for improving their classroom performance. Each contribution begins with a comment explaining the background to the activity along with a note on the intended focus. This appendix invites teachers to reflect on what they are doing, how and why they are doing it, and what they might be doing instead.

The "Mini-Recipes" in the second appendix were modelled on *haiku*, the traditional Japanese seventeen-syllable poetic form that crystallizes a moment of beauty or an intensely felt experience. These "teaching haikus" should be regarded as flashes of inspiration, each expressed in a maximum of seventeen words. It is perfectly possible to outline some excellent ideas in no more than a sentence or two. Limiting the number of words is a discipline that forces the writer to concentrate on the essential elements of an exercise and forces teachers to think out the details of how to present the activities for themselves.

A further word about the standard recipes. Paradoxically, it is often the case that the simpler the process one is describing, the more complex it becomes to describe it. I hope you will find that a good balance has been struck between the explicit and the implicit instructions. Moreover, I hope you will appreciate that the recipes were written by many different authors. Each author has an individual style and his or her own priorities regarding the different aspects of the teaching/ learning process. While a certain amount of editing has been necessary in the interests of uniformity, I hope the authors' originality and personalities remain reflected in the recipes they submitted.

I would now like to draw attention to the following miscellaneous points:

- Almost all the activities in this book require pair work or small group work at some moment or other. If there is an odd number of students in your class, simply ask the extra student to join one of the pairs or groups. In some cases this will entail minor adaptation of the task. While the groups or pairs are working, you are advised to circulate around the class, helping as necessary, offering advice and correction, and keeping students working at more or less the same pace as far as possible. Depending on the students, it may also be necessary to check that the interaction is indeed in English.
- A great deal of written work, such as writing reports or creative writing, can be done in class or assigned as homework. In some cases this is specifically mentioned, in others not.
- Much of the work on dealing with new vocabulary can be done with the aid of a dictionary, even though this is not always mentioned.
- Be careful that the activities do not go on too long. This is a particular danger in those exercises that require that something be repeated several times in some way or other. Stop the activity while student interest is still high. Do not wait for interest to wane.
- Think carefully about which activities are suitable for which classes. "Music and Memories," a nostalgic exercise about first love and music, is clearly not appropriate with a class of eight year olds.
- Be gentle when correcting students. Avoid leaving students feeling bad about themselves and "put down." Try to lead students to the correct answers through indirect correction and elicitation.
- Make a point of praising students when they try hard, do well, and get it right. The benefits of praise in motivating learners are incalculable.

I hope that the ideas contained in *More Recipes for Tired Teachers* will be passed on, personalized, and adapted. The more of yourself you put into the activities, the more you and your students will derive from them. By investing yourself in the material you can bring it to life and revitalize your classes, your colleagues, and yourself.

Sources of the activities have been cited wherever possible, although the problem of establishing originality persists. I wish to express my thanks to the authors who submitted ideas for inclusion in *More Recipes*. Without them, there would not be a book. I also thank Tab Hamlin for his advice on American usage, and my agent A. R. Evans for his assistance. A special word of gratitude is due to my wife, Kathleen, for her constant advice and encouragement.

Christopher Sion

§

ABLE OF RECIPES

Including title, author, suggested level, and appropriate time. Language functions or focus are in italics. General comments are in parentheses.

Unit I—ATTENTION AND AWARENESS

I-1 **Speaking Styles: An Awareness Session,** Dorothy Economou. High Intermediate and above. 60 minutes. *Making and evaluating judgments.* (What sort of speaker are you?) — 2

I-2 **Smells Interesting,** Marie Docherty. Intermediate and above. 20–30 minutes. *Expressing likes and dislikes, describing, recollecting, asking and answering questions.* (The power of perfume.) — 5

I-3 **Touching Icebreaker,** René Bosewitz. Intermediate and above. 10–15 minutes. *Asking and answering questions.* (Questions and answers "in the dark!" Good for group dynamics.) — 6

I-4 **The Name Icebreaker,** René Bosewitz. Intermediate to advanced. 15 minutes. *Imagining, describing.* (Do this icebreaker to find out who Amanda Schwartz is.) — 7

I-5 **Identity Swapping,** Mike Levy. Intermediate and above. 30 minutes. *Socializing.* (Getting to know each other even better.) — 8

I-6 **Chinese Proverbs,** Mike Lavery. Low intermediate and above. 15 minutes. *Speculating, discussing.* (I hear and I forget. I see and I remember. I do and I understand.) — 9

I-7 **Star-Gazing,** René Bosewitz. High intermediate and above. 30–40 minutes. *Speculating, expressing opinions.* (I'm Cancer: sensitive, protective, ... What about you?) — 10

I-8 **The Seven Deadly Sins,** Paul Docherty. Intermediate and above. 30–60 minutes. *Expressing moral preferences, making comparisons.* (Dedicated to pride, envy, lust, gluttony, anger, covetousness, and sloth.) — 12

I-9 **Grammar Drama,** Rakesh Bhanot. Intermediate. 15 minutes. *Reviewing grammar, speculating.* (Interaction within a strictly grammatical framework.) — 13

I-10 **Giving Your Friend Advice,** Frieda Paschael. Intermediate. 30 minutes. *Giving advice.* (I've got a problem. What do you advise me to do?) — 14

I-11 **The Dreaded Red Spot,** Mike Lavery. Intermediate. 30 minutes. *Persuading and denying.* (Awareness of how we allow ourselves to be distracted.) — 16

Unit II—A VISUAL BIAS

II-1 **Creative Picture Dialogue,** David Cranmer. Intermediate. 40 minutes. *Making conversation.* (Getting to the heart of a picture by writing a conversation with the people and objects depicted.) — 18

TABLE OF RECIPES (continued)

II-2   **Creative Combinations,** Claudia Kniep. Intermediate. 30 minutes. *Creative writing, describing, and inventing.* (Making creative associations between everyday objects and old masters.)   19

II-3   **Collages,** Katya Benjamin. Intermediate. 60 minutes (plus 30 minutes if you do step 5). *Asking and answering questions, explaining, making and responding to requests.* (Create a collage of your dreams and order your heart's desire from the Cosmic Waiter.)   20

II-4   **Jigsaw Advertisement,** Mike Lavery. Intermediate. 30 minutes. *Speculating, justifying.* (Presenting an ad as a jigsaw puzzle.)   21

II-5   **Picture Gallery,** Denny Packard. Elementary to advanced. 30 minutes. *Reviewing vocabulary, practicing writing.* (Reviewing vocabulary by describing a picture.)   22

II-6   **People and Pictures,** Marjorie Baudains. Intermediate. 30 minutes (plus 15 minutes for each variation in step 4). *Describing and inventing, speculating.* (Taking on the identity of a portrait.)   23

II-7   **Television Times,** René Bosewitz. Intermediate to advanced. 40 minutes. *Describing and imagining, exchanging ideas.* (Introduction to English language television.)   24

II-8   **Hide and Seek,** Randal Holme. Elementary. 15 minutes. *Giving instructions, requesting information, expressing spatial relations.* (Exciting variation of an old game.)   25

II-9   **Morning Walking,** Jeremy Smith. Beginners to advanced. 30–60 minutes. *Narrating.* (Which side of bed did you get up on this morning?)   26

Unit III—AUDITORY ACTIVITIES

III-1   **Music and Memories,** Claudia Kniep. Intermediate to advanced. 30 minutes. *Talking about the past, expressing feelings, speculating.* (Darling, they're playing our song!)   28

III-2   **Michael's Story,** Eugene Stemp. Intermediate to advanced. 60 minutes (depending on the number of students). *Narrating.* (Who said what, when?)   29

III-3   **And Now the News,** René Bosewitz. High intermediate to advanced. 60 minutes. *Passing information, note taking, summarizing.* (Students record their own news bulletin.)   31

III-4   **Like Sounds,** Loren McGrail. Intermediate. 45 minutes. *Identifying and practicing sounds.* (A medley of ideas for work on sounds.)   32

III-5   **Telephone Encounter,** Christopher Sion. Intermediate and above. 30–60 minutes. *Exchanging and comparing personal information, creative writing.* (How do you feel when the phone rings?)   34

III-6   **Fast Forward Listening,** Allan Ryding. All levels. 20 minutes. *Listening comprehension, reading for gist.* (Random intensive listening for gist.)   36

III-7   **Tune in to a Story,** Martin Rinvolucri. Intermediate. 20 minutes. *Making associations of words and music.* (Which pieces of music does a story remind you of? Can you sing them?)   37

III-8   **Ether Waiter,** Mike Levy. Low intermediate. 10 minutes. *Identifying and practicing sounds.* (Intriguing listening.)   38

Unit IV—WORKING WITH WORDS

IV-1   **Reading Comprehension,** Pat Charalambides. Intermediate to advanced. Two 60-minute lessons. *Asking and answering questions.* (Students prepare their own comprehension questions.)   40

IV-2   **Student-Centered Translation,** Martin Worth. Intermediate to advanced. 60–90 minutes. *Developing an awareness of register and the importance of context when doing translations.* (The first recipe to tackle translation.)   41

IV-3   **TV Sponsors,** René Bosewitz. Intermediate to advanced. 40 minutes. *Persuading, describing and imagining, asking and answering questions.* ($1,000,000 is at stake in this recipe!)   42

IV-4   **Stereotypes: We're Flirty, Sexy, and Dumb,** Claudia Kniep. Intermediate to advanced. 25 minutes (plus 20–30 minutes if you do step 5). *Asking and answering questions, practicing adjectives.* (Taking on new identities in order to practice adjectives.)   43

IV-5   **Categories,** Loren McGrail. Low intermediate and above. 15–30 minutes. *Categorizing vocabulary.* (Guess what category a set of words belongs to.)   44

IV-6   **Black Bags,** Dermot Murphy. High intermediate and above. 20–30 minutes. *Describing, speculating, and comparing.* (Much more than a guessing game.)   45

IV-7   **Discovery Words,** Mike Lavery. Low intermediate to advanced. 45–60 minutes. *Vocabulary acquisition.* (Selecting five unusual words to describe the picture.)   46

IV-8   **Phrasal T-Shirts: A Marketing Exercise,** Christopher Sion. High intermediate to advanced. 45–60 minutes. *Reviewing two- and three-word verbs, presenting information.* (Slogans for next year's T-shirts.)   47

IV-9   **Do-It-Yourself Cloze Test,** Marjorie Baudains. Variable. 30 minutes. *Practicing vocabulary.* (Students construct cloze tests.)   48

IV-10   **Cleanliness: A Swiss Pastime,** Margrit Wehrli. Variable. 30 minutes. *Practicing vocabulary in context.* (Useful work on grammatical and semantic awareness.)   49

Unit V—READING AND WRITING

V-1   **Conflicting Stories,** Randal Holme. Variable. Intermediate in the case of the story included here. 30 minutes. *Expressing agreement and disagreement.* (Two versions of the same story as the basis for genuine student agreement and disagreement.)   52

V-2   **Reading, Writing, and Recall,** Roy Sprenger. Intermediate to advanced. 60–90 minutes. *Making associations.* (Grouping ideas and associations into sets as the basis for writing a paragraph.)   54

V-3   **Stories by Association,** Bryan Robinson. Intermediate to advanced. Two 20–30 minute sessions. *Making associations, narrating.* (Free association plus.)   55

V-4   **Reading into a Role,** John Morgan. Variable. 15–30 minutes. *Asking and answering questions.* (Students answer questions in the roles of characters in the texts.)   56

V-5   **Silent Dialogues,** Mario Rinvolucri. Intermediate to advanced. 30–45 minutes. *Asking and answering questions, expressing opinions.* (A silent exercise builds up students' need to talk.)   58

V-6   **Dear Boss,** Martin Worth. Intermediate. 60 minutes. *Expressing preferences, voicing criticism, making suggestions.* (What would you do if you were your own boss?)   59

V-7   **Composition by Cards,** Bryan Robinson. Elementary to intermediate. 30–45 minutes. *Writing sentences, narrating.* (Creative combinations of words on cards.)   60

Unit VI—GAMES AND SIMULATIONS

VI-1   **The Human Flow Chart,** Martin Worth. High intermediate to advanced. 45–60 minutes. *Suggesting, agreeing and disagreeing, expressing opinions, presenting information.* (Students arrange themselves in the order of a sequence of logical steps.)   62

VI-2   **Student Mimes,** David Cranmer. Intermediate. 60 minutes. *Writing dialogues, speculating.* (Students mime specific situations.)   64

VI-3   **Work Expands,** Gerry Kenny. High intermediate. 20–30 minutes. *Speculating, combining words into sentences.* (Parkinson's Law.)   66

VI-4   **Outer Space Simulation,** Richard Baudains. High intermediate. 60–90 minutes. *Describing and imagining, comparing ideas.* (Two of the three planets must be depopulated . . .)   67

VI-5   **Group Dynamic Quiz,** René Bosewitz. High intermediate to advanced. 60–90 minutes. *Asking and answering questions.* (What famous event took place in Russia in 1917?)   68

VI-6   **Category Game,** Michele Meyer. Elementary to intermediate. 15–20 minutes (plus   69
20 minutes if you do step 5). *Asking and answering questions, speculating, categorizing vocabulary.* (What do donuts, continuous stationery, wash basins, and old sox have in common? [Holes!])

VI-7   **This Is my Elbow,** Sid Phipps. Intermediate. 10–15 minutes. *Reviewing vocabulary*   70
(body parts), intensive listening. (Requires intense concentration and coordination and is great fun. Try it and see!)

VI-8   **Fifteen,** Peter Schimkus. Elementary. 15–20 minutes. *Practicing numbers, calculat-*   71
ing. (Fascinating numbers game.)

VI-9   **The Roberts Family Photograph,** Ray Janssens. Intermediate. 30 minutes (plus   72
30 minutes for step 6). *Socializing, exchanging information.* (What a pity the Roberts family no longer recognizes each other.)

VI-10   **Cops and Robbers,** Dermot Murphy. Intermediate to advanced. 40–60 minutes.   75
Compiling, checking and sharing information; making and evaluating decisions; persuad-ing. (You are a U.S. police detective who must decide if Antonio Bonilla is Antonio Vargas, the well-known gangster.)

VI-11   **Fun with Headlines,** Susan Cattell and Ben Duncan. High intermediate to ad-   78
vanced. 45 minutes. *Writing newspaper headlines, agreeing and disagreeing.* (Competi-tion to match headlines and pictures.)

VI-12   **Uncle Joe's Last Fling,** Mike Perry. Intermediate. 30 minutes. *Narrating, indirect*   79
speech, expressing conditional statements, speculating. (Was Uncle Joe really on Coney Island?)

Appendix A—TEACHER DEVELOPMENT: PRACTICAL REFLECTIONS ON TEACHING

A-1   **The Iceberg,** Mike Lavery. 20–30 minutes. *Focus: Classroom awareness.* (The hidden   82
factors at work in the learning process.)

A-2   **End of Term Encounter,** Christopher Sion. 30–60 minutes. *Focus: Awareness of*   85
yourself as a teacher. (An opportunity to reflect on yourself, your students, your colleagues, and your subject.)

A-3   **Teacher's Roadworthy Test,** Mike Lavery and Christopher Sion. 20–30 minutes.   87
Focus: Revitalization of your teaching. (How many teaching miles have you done since your last teaching service?)

A-4   **Elicitation Techniques,** Christopher Sion. Time varies with the different tech-   90
niques. *Focus: Awareness that students often know far more than they are credited with.* (Simple activities that prove students are not "empty vessels waiting to be filled.")

A-5 **The Correct Balance,** Christopher Sion. Time varies with different methods. *Focus: Presenting a variety of approaches to error correction.* (Developing the teaching resources required to assist students to monitor their performance.) — 92

A-6 **Feedback: Theory and Practice,** Christopher Sion. 15–30 minutes per method. *Focus: To assist teachers develop an on-going awareness of their teaching.* (Touches on the discrepancy between what teachers and students perceive as classroom reality.) — 95

A-7 **The Writing's on the Wall,** Mike Lavery. 15–30 minutes. *Focus: Feedback.* (Becoming more aware of students' learning needs.) — 99

A-8 **Classroom Observation Checklist,** Christopher Sion. 30 minutes (not including teaching sessions observed). *Focus: Classroom observation; appraising teaching performance.* (Twenty-two points for classroom observation.) — 101

Appendix B—MINI-RECIPES

A Word of Explanation — 106

Desiring and Imagining — 107

Personal Experience — 108

Creative Writing — 109

Facts and Explanations — 110

English for Special Purposes — 111

Talking and Conversing — 112

For Teachers and Teacher Trainers — 113

Provocative and Controversial — 114

Index — 115

§

UNIT 1

ATTENTION AND AWARENESS

"Everything that irritates us about others can lead us to an understanding of ourselves."

C. G. Jung

SPEAKING STYLES: AN AWARENESS SESSION

Unit I / ATTENTION AND AWARENESS / Level: High intermediate and above / Time: 60 minutes

Language Function(s): Making and evaluating judgments

Materials: Four or five large pictures of people; copies of style *A* and style *B* speakers' styles (see page 4)

Before Class

Look for large pictures of different sorts of people, some extroverted, some introverted (one person per picture); make copies of the two speakers' styles described on page 4.

In Class

1. Draw this continuum on the board:

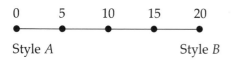

Style *A*   Style *B*

2. Distribute copies of the two styles of speaking outlined at the end of this recipe. Discuss the styles informally with the class, making sure that all the students are clear about them.

3. Divide the class into small groups. Show the students the pictures you found. Hand the pictures around if necessary to ensure that all the groups see them clearly. Tell the students their task is as follows: they should discuss where they think the people in the pictures should be placed on the continuum. Do the pictures show people who tend to be more style *A* or style *B*? As a prerequisite for step 4, all pictures should be given a score by every group.

4. Ask the groups to report back to the class. How and why did they rate the pictures as they did? Keep a record of the scores given to the pictures by each

group. In this way you can obtain the class average for each picture. If possible, display the pictures on the board along the continuum according to this average.

5. Ask the students to think about the way they speak and to place *themselves* on the continuum. They should rate themselves, first, for speaking their own language and, second, for speaking English. No one is allowed to choose 10. Anyone speaking several languages may rate them all if he or she wishes.

6. Ask the students to discuss their assessments of their speaking styles in small groups. Some students might possibly find that their classmates do not see them exactly as they see themselves. The students should decide for themselves whether, all in all, they are style *A* or style *B* speakers.

7. If you have enough time and if the situation allows, divide the class into small groups of style *A* and *B* speakers. Tell them to discuss:

   What is it like being a style *A* or style *B* speaker?
   What is it like talking to speakers of the other style?
   In what situations do the students tend to be more (or less) style *A* or style *B* speakers?
   What factors influence their speaking styles?

8. Finally, tell the class to re-form into small groups, each containing a mixture of *A* and *B* style speakers. They should tell each other what they spoke about in step 7 and, if possible, go on to discuss how their speaking styles can be made more effective.

Author's Notes

I wish to acknowledge that I got this idea from Ron West.

The notion that people's conversational styles can be placed on a continuum where style *A* is called "High Involvement" and style *B* described as "High Considerateness" may be found in: Deborah Tannen *Toward a Theory of Conversational Style: The Machine Gun Question* (Georgetown University, Sociolinguistic Working Paper No. 73).

Dorothy Economou

Editor's Note

If you have any video material of the class, perhaps filmed during a role-play or some other activity, it will be interesting to let the students view it after having completed this activity. Do the performances revealed by the video correspond with the students' perception of their speaking styles?

§

STYLE A SPEAKERS:

1. Start speaking over other people's speech. This might be intended to be helpful.

2. Continue speaking over other people's interruptions.

3. Contribute to conversations by cutting straight into others' speech without allowing a pause.

4. Have a relatively fast rate of speech.

5. Have relatively few pauses while they are speaking.

6. Prefer quite obvious changes in volume and pitch.

7. Have quite exaggerated intonation patterns.

8. Prefer personal, self-related topics.

9. Offer opinions (related or unrelated to previous talk) freely.

10. Continue contributing over a number of "turns" even when others are not responding.

STYLE B SPEAKERS:

1. Interrupt others' speech less often.

2. Tend to stop speaking in reaction to others' interruptions.

3. Allow pauses between "turns" and within their own speech.

4. Have a relatively slow rate of speech.

5. Have flatter intonation patterns.

6. Prefer impersonal, other-related topics and prefer picking up others' topics.

7. Abandon contributions not picked up by others.

8. Use hesitation and avoidance techniques more.

SMELLS INTERESTING

UNIT I / ATTENTION AND AWARENESS / Level: Intermediate and above / Time: 20–30 minutes

Language Function(s): Expressing likes and dislikes, describing, recollecting, asking and answering questions

Materials: Anything with a distinctive odor that can conveniently be brought into class

Before Class

Gather several everyday objects and substances that have distinctive smells: perfume, mature cheese, flowers, chocolate, coffee, tobacco, a used ashtray, a clove of garlic, an empty beer can, or sardine can.

In Class

1. Ask the students if they know what caused Proust to write his masterpiece, *The Remembrance of Things Past.* Either elicit from the class or, if necessary, tell them that it was "the smell of madelaine cakes." This point is intended to provide an introduction to the powerful effect of smells. Tell the class to reflect for a couple of minutes on what life would be like without a sense of smell.

2. Produce some "smelly" objects and ask the students for their reactions. The objects could be passed around the class or a few students could be asked to guess the object (with eyes closed) from the smell. Focus on language expressing personal preferences, for example: like, dislike, can't stand, hate, and adore. Give your own examples to encourage discussion as necessary. Try to get at least one response from every student.

3. Ask the students to make two columns in their notebooks and to label the columns "Pleasant" and "Un-

pleasant." Tell them to list the smells they personally like or dislike under the appropriate heading.

4. Ask the class to think about smells and recall any associations they might have of time, place, or people. Examples might include incense in church, a particular aftershave or perfume, disinfectant in a hospital, the smell of a dentist's office, baking, and so on.

5. Divide the class into pairs or small groups. Ask the students to take turns at explaining to each other why they like or dislike particular smells and what memories and associations various smells have for them. Encourage the students to describe the place, time, situation, people involved, or whatever else is connected with each smell. They should also be prepared to answer any questions that may arise.

6. As a variation for advanced classes, have the students describe a season or a place only by its smells. This could perhaps be assigned as written homework. If this proves too demanding, you can make it easier by allowing the students to use a combination of smells and sounds in their descriptions.

Marie Docherty

§

TOUCHING ICEBREAKER

Language Function(s): Asking and answering questions

Materials: Blindfolds

Before Class

1. Make sure you have enough blindfolds for the entire class. Either gather them yourself or ask the students to bring blindfolds of their own.

2. Check that the room you're teaching in is suitable for the activity. The students must be able to move around freely while blindfolded.

In Class

1. Explain the activity to the class. Tell them that you are going to ask them to put on blindfolds and then move around the room. When two students touch each other they should both ask three questions to find out something about their unknown partners. The only rule is that they may not ask questions like "What is your name?" or "Who are you?" Be sure to work through several examples so that the students are well "warmed up" when they start.

    Let's imagine, for example, that Wanda bumps into José. The blindfolds are *not* removed and Wanda asks him:

    How old are you?
    How many brothers and sisters do you have?
    What did you do last Saturday night?

José answers the questions and then it is his turn to ask Wanda three questions. For example:

    What sort of music do you like?
    Are you an optimist or a pessimist? (Why?)
    Have you read *Catch 22*?

    Tell the students that they should listen carefully to each other's voices. The object of the activity is to be able to recognize the other students by their voices once the blindfolds come off.

2. Distribute blindfolds as necessary and tell the students to proceed as described in step 1. Do not blindfold yourself. Rather act as the guide and stage manager. Move around, checking that the activity is going according to plan and helping with language difficulties as necessary.

3. After about 10 minutes ask the students to take off their blindfolds. They should now take turns telling their names to the class. If when Luigi says, "I am Luigi Cofetti," the others successfully recognize the voice, they should tell the class all they have established about him. Luigi can say whether the information is accurate. Continue around the class until everyone has had a turn.

René Bosewitz

THE NAME ICEBREAKER

Unit I / ATTENTION AND AWARENESS / Level: Intermediate to advanced / Time: 15 minutes

Language Function(s): Imagining, describing

Materials: Slips of paper

Before Class

Secure one blank slip of paper for each student in a new class in which the students do not know each other at all.

In Class

1. Distribute one slip of paper to each member of the class. Ask the students to write their full names on their slips of paper. The names should be written clearly so they are easy to read.

2. When the students are ready, collect the slips of paper and shuffle them together. Then distribute the slips at random, but making sure that nobody has his or her own name.

3. Every student now has a slip of paper with a "strange name" on it. Tell the class their task is first to imagine where the "strange name" comes from. They should then go on to supply whatever additional details they like. Tell them to be as imaginative as they can. Some suggestions are to give a physical description of the "strange name," or information relating to that person's work, hobbies, family, age, background, and experience. Tell them they have five minutes for this step.

For example, a student handed a slip of paper with the name AMANDA SCHWARTZ written on it might come up with the following profile:

> Comes from somewhere in Eastern Europe; short, stocky, with blue eyes and long dark hair; interested in medieval lute music and ice hockey; 32 years old; married with two daughters; by profession a dentist.

4. When they are finished, ask one student to tell the class the name written on his or her slip of paper. The person whose name it is should then identify himself or herself. The first student should now read out the imaginative profile that has been written. The other student, whose imaginary profile is being read out, should listen carefully and then correct and supplement the "information."

5. Continue around the class until everyone has had a turn.

René Bosewitz

§

IDENTITY SWAPPING

Unit I / ATTENTION AND AWARENESS / Level: Intermediate and above / Time: 30 minutes

Language Function(s): Socializing

Materials: A container, such as a hat or bag

In Class

1. Ask the students to write their names clearly on small pieces of paper. Then collect the pieces of paper and put them in a hat, bag, or similar container. Include your own name if you wish.

2. Tell the students to get up and move around, imagining that they are at a cocktail party. Move round the room offering imaginary drinks and snacks, introducing the "guests" to each other, and encouraging them to talk about themselves and find out about each other. This step should only last about five minutes.

3. Before the conversation begins to slacken off, take the hat around and ask each student to pick one name out of it. It is important that the students should not be able to see which name they are picking. Check that nobody has his or her own name. Tell the students to assume the identity of the person whose name they have drawn from the hat. The cocktail party can now continue with everybody role-playing the person whose name they have drawn. If you have included your own name, whoever draws it can take over the role of the host or hostess.

4. Collect the pieces of paper, let the students pick new names from the hat, and repeat step 3 with everyone playing the role of yet another member of the class. Make sure you stop well before the activity begins to run out of steam.

5. Finish off with a general discussion of the activity. The students could be divided into pairs or small groups for this task if the numbers are too large for a satisfactory whole-class discussion.

Mike Levy

Editor's Note

This activity is only suitable for well-knit classes in which the students know each other well.

§

CHINESE PROVERBS

Unit I / ATTENTION AND AWARENESS / Level: Low intermediate and above / Time: 15 minutes

Language Function(s): Speculating, discussing

Materials: None

In Class

1. Write the three proverbs listed below on the board:

   > I do and I forget;
   > I hear and I remember;
   > I see and I understand.

   > I see and I forget;
   > I do and I remember;
   > I hear and I understand.

   > I hear and I forget;
   > I see and I remember;
   > I do and I understand.

2. Divide the class into pairs or small groups. Tell the class that only one of the three proverbs is a genuine old Chinese saying. The students have a double task: first, they should discuss the proverbs; second, they should speculate on which of the three is the genuine proverb. (By the way, which do *you* think is genuine? The answer can be found at the beginning of the next step.)

3. The third proverb is the genuine Chinese saying. An optional extra step is to ask the students to discuss the relevance of this proverb to the learning of a foreign language. The proverb concisely sums up the importance of the visual dimension of memory and the effectiveness of learning by doing. These are important aspects in the process of "learning how to learn" that some students may not be aware of.

Mike Lavery

§

 **S**TAR-GAZING

Unit I / ATTENTION AND AWARENESS / Level: High intermediate and above / Time: 30–40 minutes

Language Function(s): Speculating, expressing opinions

Materials: An astrology column from a newspaper or magazine

Before Class

Check that the language in the astrology column is at a suitable level for your class; cut up the column so that each sign is separate.

In Class

1. Distribute the 12 signs you have cut up to the class. In small classes, some students may be given more than one sign. In larger classes, students may have to work in pairs or threes. Tell the students to study the signs they have been given. Circulate as they read, providing help with the language as necessary.

2. Ask the students to read the slips of paper one by one to the class. Help them with the pronunciation and intonation and write the name of each sign on the board as it occurs.

3. Now ask the students to suggest the typical characteristics of each constellation, for example: Aries—aggressive, full of ideas, stubborn. If possible, elicit the characteristics of all the signs from the students and write them on the board. If the students don't know the characteristics, help them with information from the list following this recipe.

4. Once the characteristics have been established, ask the students to try to guess on the basis of the information on the board which signs of the zodiac the other members of the class were born under.

5. Finish the session with a discussion of the validity of horoscopes and astrology. Be prepared for a lively exchange of views: while many students are likely to be skeptical, others will be convinced that "there is something in it" or will read their horoscopes in the popular press despite their better judgment.

Author's Note

Since this recipe requires that the students know each other reasonably well, it's probably best done toward the end of a course or school year. Be sure to handle the activity gently; remember that having students express opinions about what sort of people their classmates are could be painful to some of them if not dealt with tactfully.

René Bosewitz

§

Characteristics of Signs of the Zodiac*

Capricorn (December 22–January 20)
Ambitious, know where they are going, but can become negative and lacking in self-confidence. Cautious, reserved, musical. Dry sense of humor.

Aquarius (January 21–February 18)
Individualistic, original, and idealistic. Inventive, helpful, and loyal. Good mixers but unconventional and unpredictable. "Private people."

Pisces (February 19–March 20)
Dreamers. Inconsistent. Can become deceitful to avoid tricky situations. They find the caring professions and artistic activities most satisfying.

Aries (March 21–April 20)
Positive, masculine, extrovert, selfish, and careless. People born under Aries are leaders, winners, "me-first people."

Taurus (April 21–May 21)
Steadfast, reliable, loving, enjoyers of the good things of life. Progressive, persistent, and practical with a lot of common sense.

Gemini (May 22–June 21)
Versatile, lively, communicative, intellectually stimulating. Restless, often leaving tasks unfinished as they switch from one interest to another.

Cancer (June 22–July 22)
Sensitive, protective, imaginative, and intuitive. Good memory. Strongly attached to home and family. Moody, emotional, and prone to worry.

Leo (July 23–August 23)
Big-hearted, bossy, and optimistic. Enthusiastic, with expensive taste and a great sense of drama. Leos make good managers and organizers.

Virgo (August 24–September 22)
Modest, charming, shy, energetic, and hard-working. Particularly like serving others. Logical, analytic, and critical.

Libra (September 23–October 23)
Need to share their lives and find balance and harmony. Peace-loving, charming, diplomatic, and hard-suffering. Indecisive and resentful.

Scorpio (October 24–November 22)
Powerful emotional and physical resources. Need to direct their energy in rewarding directions. Difficult for them to talk about their problems.

Sagittarius (November 23–December 21)
Deep need for freedom. Enthusiastic and versatile with a flair for languages. Enjoy a challenge. Eternal students. Blindly optimistic.

---

*Summarized from J. Parker "Signs of the Zodiac" (Webb & Bower, England)

THE SEVEN DEADLY SINS

Unit I / ATTENTION AND AWARENESS / Level: Intermediate and above / Time: 30–60 minutes

Language Function(s): Expressing moral preferences, making comparisons

Materials: Glossy magazines, if you try the option described in step 3c

In Class

1. Tell the class you want to deal with the "Seven Deadly Sins" and elicit what they are from the students as far as possible. The list reads: pride, envy, lust, gluttony, anger, covetousness, and sloth. Make sure that all the members of the class understand the vocabulary.

2. Ask the students, working individually, to rank order the Seven Deadly Sins from most sinful to least sinful. Ask them to discuss their rankings in pairs or small groups when they have finished. This may well lead on to a general discussion involving the whole class.

3. Continue in any of the following ways:

   a. Have the students construct short dialogues to illustrate "the wicked ways of the world." These could take the form of miniature morality plays. The students may work alone, in pairs, or in small groups. They then present their dialogues to the whole class.

   b. Divide the class into groups. Each group is to mime a situation depicting one or two of the Seven Deadly Sins. The other students have to try and guess which sins are being presented. The stories presented in the mimes could then be written, possibly as a homework exercise, with particular attention being paid to "The moral of the story."

   c. Bring some glossy magazines into class. Distribute the magazines to the students and tell them to flip through the magazines, looking at the advertisements. Their task is to try and analyze which of the Seven Deadly Sins is being appealed to by the advertisements. With advanced classes you can finish the lesson with a general discussion of a related topic such as "Values in the Modern World."

Author's Note

I wish to acknowledge that I learned the idea expressed in step 3c from Cynthia Beresford.

Paul Docherty

§

GRAMMAR DRAMA

Unit I / ATTENTION AND AWARENESS / Level : Intermediate / Time: 15 minutes

Language Function(s): Reviewing grammar, speculating

Materials: Postcard-size cards

Before Class

Think of some grammatical structures you want to review, for example: future with *going to*, degrees of comparison, simple past. Write these structures clearly on small cards. You need one for every member of the class. Each card should have one structure written on it.

In Class

1. Check through the list of structures you have selected, making sure that all students understand what you mean by the terminology. Do not assume that your class will know what a "gerund" or the "past perfect" is. Elicit several examples of each structure so that everyone is clear about them.

2. Divide the class into groups of about six students, preferably seated in circles. Give each student a card with one of the structures written on it. In any group, all students should have cards with different structures on them. The students should *not* tell each other what their structures are.

3. Give each group a topic to discuss. Simple examples are making plans for a weekend or holiday, organizing fund-raising activities for a charity, or planning a child's birthday party. In fact, the topic can be anything at all, although it is obviously best to find some-

thing that the groups are interested in. The topics may vary from group to group.

4. Tell the groups to hold their discussions as follows: The students are to make as many statements as they can using the structure they have been given on their cards.

   For example, Roberta's card says "Present Perfect" and Yoko has "First Conditional." They are told to discuss "Going on an excursion." Roberta may begin: "I haven't been on an excursion for ages. I haven't been out of town since we built the swimming pool." Yoko's contribution may start: "If we go on a long excursion, we'll have to think about lunch. If we go sightseeing, I must remember to take my camera."

5. Help the students as necessary, letting them correct each other as far as possible. After about five minutes, tell the groups to stop their discussions. The students should now say which structures they think the others have been using.

6. If interest permits, have the students swap cards, give them some new discussion topics, and let them repeat the activity.

Rakesh Bhanot

GIVING YOUR FRIEND ADVICE

Language Function(s): Giving advice

Materials: Small pieces of card (preferably two colors) *or* copies of page 15 glued onto thin cardboard

Before Class

Copy the problems following this recipe (page 15) onto cards, one problem or one piece of advice per card. It is a good idea to use one color for the problem cards and another color for the advice cards. If you have easy access to a photocopier, another possibility is to copy the whole of page 15, glue it to a piece of thin card, and then cut it into separate problems and pieces of advice.

In Class

1. Write an example of a problem on the board and then teach the class some ways of giving advice. Key phrases here are "I think you should . . . ," "Why don't you try . . . ?" "I suggest . . . ," "If I were you . . . ," and so on.

    For example, if the problem is "I have a tooth-ache," suitable advice is:

    I think you should go to the dentist.
    Have you thought about making a dental
      appointment?
    I suggest you stop eating so much candy.
    If I were you I'd take an aspirin.
    Why don't you take something for it?

2. Ask five students to come to the front of the class-room and give each of them one of the problem cards. Distribute the advice cards among the rest of the students.

3. Ask the students at the front, one by one. "What's the matter with you?" For example, the one who has the card saying "A cough" will say, "I have a cough." The rest of the class should use their cards as the basis for giving advice on dealing with coughs. Encourage the class to use forms like those included in step 1: "Why don't you suck a cough drop?" "If I were you I'd give up smoking." The student at the front can decide whether to accept or reject the advice.

4. With really well-knit classes you can try asking the students if they have any minor problems of their own that they would be prepared to discuss with the class. The class should try to find a sensible solution to the problem and give the advice using the appropriate language. To set this phase in motion, it is a good idea to volunteer a problem or dilemma of your own. Whatever you do, don't force the students to discuss personal problems if they are unwilling to.

Author's Note

This is an extended version of an article which originally appeared in *Modern English Teacher* (Vol. 10, No. 1).

Frieda Paschael

WHAT'S THE MATTER WITH YOU?

A headache

Take two aspirins.

See a doctor.

Go to bed.

Sit quietly.

Walk in the fresh air.

Drink less alcohol.

Relax.

A sore foot

Rest it.

Put it in cold water.

Bandage it.

Use a walking stick.

Put ointment on it.

Take off your shoe.

Sit down.

A cough

Stop smoking.

Suck a cough drop.

Take an aspirin.

Drink some honey and lemon.

See a doctor.

Buy some cough mixture.

Go to the pharmacy.

A backache

Lie flat.

See a specialist.

Have some heat treatment.

Sit on a straight chair.

Do some light exercise.

Avoid lifting heavy weights.

Have a massage.

Overweight

Eat less.

Take more exercise.

Run every day.

Go on diet.

Eat only vegetables.

Avoid eating sugar.

Eat less bread.

I-11 THE DREADED RED SPOT

Language Function(s): Persuading and denying

Materials: Small round adhesive spots or colored felt-tipped pens

The goal of this activity is to foster awareness of how we allow ourselves to be distracted.

In Class

1. Divide the class into two groups, *A* and *B*. Tell group *A* to think up some discussion topics and to prepare some points to discuss with group *B*. The topics can be about anything but should be of general interest. Tell them they have about five minutes.

2. As group *A* begins, take group *B* out of the room and ask the members to put a colored spot on their faces, using the felt-tipped pens or small adhesive spots. Tell them that when they return to the classroom they should each find a partner from group *A* to talk to. Should the partners comment on the spots, the group *B* students concerned should dismiss the remarks as being nonsense. They should absolutely deny the existence of the spots and should make a mental note of their partners' reactions and arguments.

3. While group *B* is getting ready, return to group *A* and check that all is well. Tell them that when their classmates return they should start up a conversation with them on one of the topics they have been preparing. During the conversation they should keep their hands folded behind their backs.

4. Ask the "spotted students" to come in and find partners from group *A*. You might find it effective to play some lively background music to help break down inhibitions. Let the pairs talk for three to five minutes. Circulate around the class, helping as necessary and making notes of any language problems for analysis at a later date.

5. Have the class reassemble and ask the students to reconstruct their conversations orally. Could they remember exactly what was said? How did group *A* react to group *B*'s spots? Did they manage to keep their hands behind their backs? Share any observations that you made.

Author's Note

You can also do the exercise with three groups of students where the third group's task is to act as observers. This means, of course, that you have to brief this third group separately.

Mike Lavery

§

UNIT II

VISUAL BIAS

"If I am supposed to describe how an object looks from far off, I don't make the description more accurate by saying what can be noticed about the object on closer inspection."

Ludwig Wittgenstein

CREATIVE PICTURE DIALOGUE

Unit II / A VISUAL BIAS / Level: Intermediate / Time: 40 minutes

Language Function(s): Making conversation

Materials: None

Before Class

Arrange the seats in a semicircle around the board. Make sure there is no physical object (like the teacher's desk) between the students and the board as this could inhibit the class from doing the task described in step 2.

In Class

1. Ask the class to sit in the semicircle of seats you have arranged. Be prepared to join in the semicircle yourself.

2. Either draw an object on the board or ask one of the students to draw something simple. Then ask other students to come to the front and add further objects to the picture until the board is full but uncluttered. About ten items should be right. There needn't be any obvious connection between the drawings, although there often is. You might begin with a tree. Students tend to respond by adding people, animals, birds, a house, the sun, and so on.

3. Ask the students to write a dialogue between any two of the objects or people in the picture. They can work alone or in pairs. In the case of the following picture, possible conversations would be between the fish and the boat, the house and the sun, or one of the children and the water. Each student (or pair) should write one dialogue.

4. When the students begin, you should move outside the semicircle, well out of the way, for a few minutes. This leaves the students unpressured while they decide what they want to write. When you decide that the time is right, return to the semicircle and provide vocabulary and other help as necessary and gently correct any errors.

5. Ask the students to read their dialogues to the class. Allow them time to answer any questions that arise. Another possibility is for the students to make neat copies of their dialogues and display them on the classroom walls for everyone to read after class at their leisure. If interest permits, finish the lesson with a discussion of why students chose the objects they did.

Author's Note

The technique of building up a group picture is from *Once Upon a Time* by John Morgan and Mario Rinvolucri (Cambridge University Press, 1983).

David Cranmer

§

CREATIVE COMBINATIONS

Unit II / A VISUAL BIAS / Level: Intermediate / Time: 30 minutes

Language Function(s): Creative writing, describing, and inventing

Materials: Reproductions of famous paintings and small cards—one reproduction and one card per student

Before Class

Choose a few reproductions of pre-twentieth century paintings. Postcard size is ideal. Write the names of some modern objects or appliances on the cards. Good examples are vacuum cleaner, sports car, television set, and typewriter.

In Class

1. Give every student one picture and one card at *random*. Tell them to make a story that links the two elements in whatever way they want. You can give an example first if you wish, although this is not altogether necessary. Move around the class, providing help as required. Correct the students' language only when a suitable moment presents itself. Be careful not to break abruptly into a student's train of thought. On no account should your corrections cramp the students' style.

2. The activity proceeds as follows: One by one, the students should show their pictures to the class, passing them around if necessary to make sure that everyone has seen them. The students should say what the words on their cards are as they take turns reading their stories to the class. If you have a large class, divide the students into groups or the activity will take too long. If you have a competitive class, you can finish the lesson by asking the students to vote which was the best story.

Author's Note

To give an idea of the sort of work you can expect, I should like to include two stories written by students of mine:

"Malle Babbe" (by Frans Hals) and a typewriter:

In this picture I can see a woman. She has a pot of beer in her hand and an owl on her shoulder. She is laughing and is looking around for a typewriter because she wants to write a letter to her husband to tell him how happy she is.

"John the Baptist" (by Geertgen tot Sint Jans) and an airplane:

John the Baptist is sitting on a big stone. He is a little bored because nothing is happening at the moment. But soon an aircraft will arrive with many people on board. John the Baptist will baptize them in the little river I can see in the background.

Claudia Kniep

§

Unit II / A VISUAL BIAS / Level: Intermediate / Time: 60 minutes plus 30 minutes if you do step 5

Language Function(s): Asking and answering questions, explaining, making and responding to requests

Materials: Old magazines containing a good selection of different pictures suitable for cutting out, pairs of scissors, glue, large sheets of cardboard, thumbtacks or other suitable means of fixing cardboard to the wall

Before Class

Secure the materials. If you have a large class, it is advisable to ask students to bring their own scissors and paste.

In Class

1. Distribute the materials. Tell the students you want them to leaf through the magazines and make a collage. The students should cut out any pictures or slogans (or anything else) they want and paste these items onto their sheets of cardboard. The collages should reflect what the students want from their lives. Leave them free to interpret this in their own ways but point out that they can focus on the symbolic as well as the representational side of the pictures. A beautiful country house may be seen as a pleasant place to live or as a symbol of peace and security. Suggest that the students include a short written explanation of their collages. These should be pasted onto the cardboard alongside the pictures.

2. Go around the class while the students work. Ask the students questions about the significance of their collages and help them with any language problems as necessary. It is very effective to play some music *quietly* in the background as the activity progresses.

3. After a while, tell the students they are free to mill around the room informally. Let them discuss and explain their collages to each other in small groups.

As the students will finish their collages at different times, some can be circulating while the others continue working.

4. When all the collages have been finished they can be exhibited around the classroom. This provides the students with a further opportunity to look at their classmates' work and allows them to spend some more time asking and answering questions about the collages.

5. An excellent follow-up to "Collages" is "The Cosmic Waiter."

   a. Ask the class to cut out some more pictures and use them to build up a substantial central picture bank.

   b. Divide the class into pairs. Explain that the partners in each pair will take turns at being the waiter and the customer. Tell the students that the customers can order anything they desire, absolutely anything at all!

   c. The waiters are to note the customers' orders and then go and try to find pictures of them in the picture bank. The customers can then be served.

   d. Customers should now explain to the waiters why they want what they have ordered. If the articles are not in the bank, the waiter can offer an alternative or ask if there is something else the customer would prefer.

Author's Note

I wish to acknowledge that this contribution has been influenced by "Rebirthing Techniques."

Katya Benjamin

§

20

JIGSAW ADVERTISEMENT

Unit II / A VISUAL BIAS / Level: Intermediate / Time: 30 minutes

Language Function(s): Speculating, justifying

Materials: An advertisement, glue, cardboard, scissors

Before Class

Select an advertisement where the product has no obvious connection with the illustration, for example a picture of a waterfall advertising cigarettes. Mount it on cardboard and then cut it into about ten pieces.

In Class

1. Give the class one piece of the jigsaw puzzle you have made. Make sure it is not a piece that would immediately disclose what the ad is for. Tell the students it is part of an advertisement. Have them pass it round and ask them to speculate about what product or service the ad is promoting. Ask a class "secretary" to write the speculations on the board.

2. Give the students the remaining pieces of the puzzle one by one. Ask them to continue speculating and also to justify their ideas. Don't tell them at this stage whether they are right or wrong. Only when the puzzle has been completed will the students finally see what the advertisement is for.

3. Ask the students to choose one item each from the list the class secretary has written on the board. Next ask them to draw or describe a possible advertising picture for that product or service. It should be one that has no direct connection with the product. For example, a beach with a solitary palm tree may be chosen to advertise furniture, or a bicycle to promote computers.

4. The students show their drawings or read their descriptions to the rest of the class, whose task is now to speculate about which of the products and services on the board is being referred to. The class should justify their speculations. The students should then identify the product or service they had in mind and explain their drawings or descriptions. It's a good idea to finish the activity by suggesting that the students try to imagine a catch phrase or slogan that the advertiser might use to connect the picture and the product.

Mike Lavery

§

ICTURE GALLERY

Unit II / A VISUAL BIAS / Level: Elementary to advanced / Time: 30 minutes

Language Function(s): Reviewing vocabulary, practicing writing

Materials: 12 to 15 varied pictures or photographs with strong visual elements, thumbtacks or some other convenient means of sticking the pictures around the room; you need a room which allows the students to move around easily

Before Class

Mount the pictures on the walls around the class.

In Class

1. Ask the students to make a list of at least six words they have trouble remembering or have learned during the past week. (This may be assigned as homework to be taken up at the following lesson.)

2. Tell the students to wander round the class looking at the pictures. Each student should mentally select one picture to work with and then return to his or her seat without saying which picture it is. It does not matter if some pictures are chosen by more than one student. In fact this invariably happens, no matter what the size of the class.

3. Tell the class that each student is to write one paragraph about the picture he or she has chosen and incorporate at least five of the words on his or her list. The students should underline these words. As the students work, move around the class, providing assistance or suggesting improvements as necessary.

4. Ask the students to work in small groups. Allow them to take turns at reading their stories while the others in their group try to guess which pictures they wrote about.

5. When the groups have all finished, tell the students to write their names on their paragraphs and then stick them on the wall next to the relevant pictures. Tell the students to circulate and read the compositions written by their classmates. Any student may be called on to answer questions, explain how they chose their lists of words, and say how they plan to remember them. Suggest that the students make agreements with each other to check that they have remembered their words the following day.

Author's Note

This activity is basically a synthesis of "Picture Gallery" from John Morgan and Mario Rinvolucri's "Vocabulary" (OUP) and "Story from Words" in Melville, *et al. Towards the Creative Teaching of English* (Heinemann).

Denny Packard

§

PEOPLE AND PICTURES

Unit II / A VISUAL BIAS / Level: Intermediate / Time: 30 minutes plus 15 minutes for each variation in step 4

Language Function(s): Describing and inventing, speculating

Materials: Portraits cut from newspapers or magazines, thumbtacks or other suitable means of sticking the portraits around the class; you need a room in which students can move around freely; suitable video sequences, video recorder and monitor if you do step 4c

Before Class

Cut several clear portraits from some newspapers or magazines. The portraits will most probably be photographs, although drawings (such as caricatures) can also be used. Set up the video equipment if you are doing step 4c.

In Class

1. Exhibit the portraits around the room and ask the students to circulate and select one each. Tell the students they should imagine themselves taking on the identity of the person whose portrait they have chosen.

2. Arrange the class in pairs or small groups. The students should role-play the people in the portraits they have selected. In other words, tell the students to talk to each other as if they were the people in the portraits. What is the story of their new character? What is the person doing? Who is he or she talking to? What is the background to the portrait? For example, is it set at a wedding, business lunch, conference, ball game, tennis match, etc.?

3. Ask the students to discuss their stories. Did the stories seem to be appropriate and convincing or were they contrived? Can anyone create a better story?

4. Variations:

   a. Tell the class to change partners. The students should work in pairs, but not with someone they worked with in step 2. Their task is to retell the story or stories they have been told.

   b. Tell the students to write the stories they have created. This can be done in class or assigned as homework.

   c. Instead of the portraits you can use extracts from television programs or short scenes from a dramatic episode in a film or video with the volume turned down so that the soundtrack cannot be heard.

Marjorie Baudains

§

TELEVISION TIMES

Unit II / A VISUAL BIAS / Level: Intermediate to advanced / Time: 40 minutes

Language Function(s): Describing and imagining, exchanging ideas

Materials: List of television programs taken from an English language newspaper or TV guide, a large clock with hands that are easy to turn or a digital clock that is simple to operate

Before Class

Cut the list of one day's television programs from the newspaper or TV guide. Select the four most important channels and cut out these four channels' programs separately. (If one program is printed on the back of another, make a copy of one side of the page.)

In Class

1. Divide the class into four groups corresponding to the four most important TV channels. Give each group a copy of the programs for one of the channels. As the channels will vary from country to country, let's call them Channels 1, 2, 3 and 4 for convenience.

2. Set the clock to any time, perhaps closing your eyes as you do, and call out the name of one of the channels. This task could also be done by one of the students. For example, typical combinations would be: "9:30 a.m.–Channel 3" or "3:15 p.m.–Channel 2." Give all four groups a time in this way.

3. The group whose channel has been named should consult their programs and say what program would be broadcast at the time specified. It might be anything from mud wrestling to modern dance or current affairs. Should the clock have landed on a time when nothing is being broadcast on a particular channel, try again until a suitable time is found.

4. Tell the groups to discuss what they think their respective programs are about. Even if they have no idea at all, they should simply use their imaginations, which is all part of the fun.

5. Have the groups present their ideas to the class. This could be in the form of a description, or the groups could act their ideas in short extemporaneous performances if the programs permit. (One group may have a five-minute comedy spot, another "Gone with the Wind.")

6. Repeat the activity with other times if time and interest allow. Make sure you don't go on too long, or the students' attention will begin to wander.

Author's Note

If your area does not have four TV channels, the activity could easily be adapted to three or two channels. The activity as described here is not suitable for one channel.

René Bosewitz

Editor's Note

If you are in an English speaking country and your students have access to television, this activity could be used as a valuable lead-in to actually watching some of the programs that have been discussed.

§

HIDE AND SEEK

Unit II / A VISUAL BIAS / Level: Elementary / Time: 15 minutes

Language Function(s): Giving instructions, requesting information, expressing spatial relations

Materials: Lots of pictures of objects; you also need a classroom which allows the students to move around freely

Before Class

Collect pictures of objects at an appropriate level for your class.

In Class

1. Divide the class into pairs and give several pictures of objects to each pair. Check that the pairs know the English words for the objects shown in the pictures.

2. Tell the students that one student in each pair (the hiders) should take the pictures and hide them (face down) around the room. They should make a note of where the pictures are. The others (the seekers) should shut their eyes during this phase.

3. When the pictures have been hidden, the hiders should return to their seats. Once the students are all seated again, tell the class that the object of the exercise is to find the pictures as quickly as possible, with the hiders guiding their partners (the seekers). The hiders should avoid pointing or making any other gestures. They should restrict themselves to giving verbal instructions. The seekers may ask questions. It is advisable to have a short demonstration so that everybody is quite clear about what they are required to do. A typical exchange would be as follows:

Hider: The picture of the candle is behind one of the drapes.
Seeker: At the front of the room?
Hider: No, not at the front.
Seeker: I can see it's not at the back of the room. It must be in the middle. (Goes to the window in the middle and finds picture of the candle.) Eureka! What's next?
Hider: Well done! The next object is a goldfish bowl. You can find it on the floor.
Seeker: Is it on my left or my right as I'm standing now? (And so on.)

4. The hiders give the seekers instructions and follow them around the classroom as the seekers hunt for the pictures and collect them as they find them. It is a good idea to set a time limit within which the pictures have to be found so that the activity moves along briskly. About five minutes should be enough. Once the activity is underway there will probably be considerable noise and confusion. This is really quite valuable as it helps break down the students' inhibitions and encourages them to listen closely and express themselves with care. Move round the room as the activity continues, helping as necessary and making sure that the lesson doesn't get out of control.

Randal Holme

§

# MORNING WALKING

Language Function(s): Narrating

Materials: Overhead projector, screen, transparencies and pens for writing on transparencies. (If projection equipment is not available, use large sheets of paper and thick felt-tipped pens.)

Before Class

Secure the materials and set them up in the classroom. Check that the overhead projector is working.

In Class

1. To warm the class up, ask the students to tell you what they did this morning. Elicit a couple of examples from all the students. This step should not take more than about five minutes. If you are working with beginners who have not yet learned the past simple tense, use the present simple instead and ask them to tell you what they do every morning. Adapt the following steps of the recipe accordingly.

2. Give each student an overhead projector transparency and pen.

3. Divide the class into pairs. Let's call the students in each pair *A* and *B*. Ask the *A*'s to give the *B*'s a detailed account of their movements from waking up to leaving home. As the *A*'s talk, they should put the point of their pen on a transparency and move it to illustrate their movements. For example, "I got out of bed and opened the window. Then I walked round the bed to the bedroom door . . ." would be drawn something like this:

Tell the students not to lift their pens from the transparencies. They should not write any words, nor should they directly draw any walls, doors, furniture, etc. These objects will only be present invisibly, by inference.

4. When the *A*'s have finished, tell them to sign their drawings and hand them to you. Then tell the pairs to repeat the exercise, this time with the *B*'s drawing and the *A*'s listening. The *B*'s transparencies should also be signed and collected once they have been completed.

5. Place one of the transparencies on the overhead projector. Ask the partner of the student who did the drawing to come to the front of the class and recall the movements shown on the transparency. The student who did the drawing should correct inaccuracies, supply additional information and answer other students' questions as necessary.

6. Repeat the procedure described in step 5 until all the drawings have been displayed and described.

7. An amusing variation with which to finish "Morning Walking" is to put the transparencies on the projector one by one and ask the class if the drawings resemble anything. If necessary, turn the transparencies upside down or on their sides.

Author's Note

This activity is particularly valuable for practicing verbs such as *wash, shave,* and *dress,* which are reflexive in many other languages.

Jeremy Smith

§

UNIT III

AUDITORY ACTIVITIES

"... the sincere controversialist is above all things a good listener. The really burning enthusiast never interrupts."

G. K. Chesterton

USIC AND MEMORIES

Language Function(s): Talking about the past, expressing feelings, speculating

Materials: A cassette recorder, a cassette recording of a song that deals with first love, copies of the text of the song (if possible)

Before Class

Choose a song, prepare a cassette recording of it and make copies of the text if you have it. Good songs are "Crocodile Rock" by Elton John, "Me and Bobby McGee" by Janis Joplin, Bob Seger singing "Against the Wind" or Dooley Wilson's version of "As Time Goes By" from the film *Casablanca*.

In Class

1. Play the song, explain the meaning of the words, and, if you have them, give out copies of the text. Repeat the song once or twice to set the mood and so that students become familiar with it. It's a good idea to continue playing it softly, as background music, while the students carry on with the activity.

2. Tell the class to close their eyes and think about music and memories and the way music can "bring back" people and places. Give the students a couple of minutes to sit quietly listening to the music and reminiscing. They need a little time to "warm up."

3. Divide the class into pairs or small groups of students who feel comfortable working together. This is very important because of the personal nature of the discussion topics.

4. Write the following list of points on the board and ask the students to discuss them. Tell them to provide as much background as they feel comfortable with. Monitor the proceedings carefully as the students start their discussions. Provide help as necessary.

   What are your favorite pieces of music, the music that's really closest to you?
   Do you have a special song?
   Can you remember your first dance?
   If so, who did you dance with? Can you remember what music was playing?
   Can you remember your first love? What happened to him or her? What would have happened if you had stayed together?

5. Ask the students if anyone would like to share their own reminiscences with the whole class. Do *not* tell students to report back to the class what their partners have told them, as this would be a breach of confidence.

Author's Note

If you set this activity up tactfully, you'll find it extremely rewarding. I found a faraway look came to people's faces when discussing these questions. They brought up vivid pictures of swing bands, ballrooms, and juke-boxes. The first loves ranged from the "one-week-fling" to the heartbreaking ending and the once-in-a-lifetime love. One man had even married his sweetheart!

Claudia Kniep

§

**UNIT III / AUDITORY ACTIVITIES / Level: Intermediate to advanced /
Time: 60 minutes (depending on the number of students)**

Language Function(s): Narrating

Materials: Cassette recorder, blank cassette, copies of a story

Before Class

1. Select a story and make copies of it. Either use the story on page 30 or find one of the same length which is of particular relevance to your class. Choose a story that does not contain any new vocabulary.

2. Show one student how to operate the recorder using the pause button. (This student will be referred to as the class "audio engineer.")

3. Set the recorder on "record" so that it is being held by the pause button. Check that the recorder is recording. (If your recorder has no pause button, the recorder will have to be operated by stopping and starting the recording function itself.)

In Class

1. Explain the activity to the class. Tell them that you are going to send all the students except A and the audio engineer out of the room. They will be called back one by one to hear a story. They should listen carefully as they will have to retell the story.

2. Send all the students except A and the audio engineer out of the room. Read the story to A twice so that he or she has a fair chance to grasp the main points. The audio engineer should record one of the two readings. Tell A that you are now going to call B into the room. A should retell the story to B. A should tell the story (once only) and the audio engineer should record it.

3. Call B into the classroom. Repeat that A is going to tell B a story. Warn B to listen carefully because he or she will be required to retell the story later. Then A tells B the story (once only) and the audio engineer records it.

4. A now leaves the classroom. C goes in and B tells C the story. Continue like this until the last student, Z, has heard the story from Y. The audio engineer records the story each time it is told.

5. Tell the class to reassemble. Play the whole set of recordings from the beginning, telling the students to note the details which have been omitted and retained and any changes in the storyline. These points can be discussed in pairs, small groups, or as a whole-class task. After a few minutes, distribute copies of the original story for reference.

6. Finish off with a discussion of why omissions and changes occur and why some details, such as colors, remain intact.

Author's Note

This activity is based on a psychological experiment. The conclusion was that the brain retains and highlights certain details from a story and then reconstructs new stories around those details.

Eugene Stemp

Editor's Note

If you have more than a dozen students in your class, pick out about six of the better ones to do the activity. Proceed exactly as described above but tell the rest of the class to observe. This will prevent the activity from running too long.

§

Michael's Story

The sun was shining when we went to see Michael. He was visiting his grandfather who lives on Chestnut Street.

He was nine years old and was a small boy for his age. That day he was wearing a red sweater and faded denims.

His mother was also there. She welcomed us and we had tea and cookies. Michael had a coloring book and was uninterested in our arrival. He was busy coloring a cow green.

Michael's mother played a record of French folk songs. The music played quietly as we drank our tea and ate some delicious cream cakes.

When the music finished, Michael's mother told him to go to the piano and play. Michael did not want to at first, but when his mother insisted he stood up and went to the piano.

He played the music exactly as we had heard it; not only the tune, but the incidental frills as well. His movements were convulsed and frenzied.

When he had finished the piece, he sat down and continued his drawing.

AND NOW THE NEWS III-3

Language Function(s): Passing information, note taking, summarizing

Materials: Cassette recorder, recording of a short radio news bulletin

Before Class

Record a short bulletin of news in English from the radio. Ideally it should contain about six to eight items. If appropriate news broadcasts in English are not available to you, create your own and make a recording of it. Use a newspaper for reference.

In Class

1. Write the news items contained in the broadcast on the board in headline style; for example: "Drought Worsens," "President's Latest Gaffe," "More Money for the Contras?" etc.

2. Divide the class into pairs. Tell the students you are going to play them a recording of the news bulletin which contains the items written on the board. Ask the pairs to select one of the items before they hear the recording. It is best if each pair has one item, but depending on the numbers in your class, it might be necessary to have some students working alone or in threes.

3. Play the complete broadcast through once without a break. Then repeat it, telling the pairs to focus on the items they have selected. Tell the students to take notes of the contents of their news items. Discuss new vocabulary at an appropriate opportunity. Repeat the individual items or the whole broadcast as you think fit.

4. Tell the students they should now spend a few minutes discussing their news items with their partners. They should swap notes with their partners and should prepare an outline of the content of their items. Tell them they should prepare to retell their items as if they were newscasters. Circulate, helping as necessary.

5. Ask the pairs to regroup. One student in each pair should be the spokesperson. The task is to reconstruct and present the news, item by item. The students are often able to lift the detailed lexis and structural material used in the news directly into their reconstructions.

6. Play the recording of the news one last time.

7. Finally, tell the students to make a fair copy of their outlines. This could either be done in class or assigned as homework.

René Bosewitz

§

III-4 LIKE SOUNDS

Unit III / AUDITORY ACTIVITIES / Level: Intermediate / Time: 45 minutes

Language Function(s): Identifying and practicing sounds

Materials: None

Before Class

Prepare a list of about 15 pairs of words of one syllable that can be matched according to their vowel sounds, for example:

give/this	how/bout	few/use
son/run	shoe/blue	wait/late
voice/boy	leave/these	wood/could
said/yes	goes/know	might/cry
cat/back	John/stop	off/all

In Class

1. Scatter the words over the board in any order. Ask the students to pronounce any word(s) they are not sure of. Tell them you will pronounce the words correctly after they have made their attempts. Tell the students you will repeat the correct pronunciation for them if they wish, but each time they request a word *they* must pronounce the words themselves first. You are a sort of "human computer." Stand behind the student you are helping so that he or she cannot see you but can only hear your voice as he or she focuses on the sounds.

2. Arrange the class in groups of three or four. Ask the students to try and find the groups of matching sounds. While the students work, move quietly behind them, offering help with pronunciation only when asked. Again, the students must speak first.

3. When the groups have finished, ask each student to write one or two of the pairs of words on the board. Note that some of the words may have been incorrectly matched. Read out all the pairs in a neutral tone. If there are mistakes the students should be able to hear them from your pronunciation. It should not be necessary to draw their attention to the mistakes directly. If the mistakes go unnoticed, you might indicate *where* the problem is, but without giving away *what* it is. Only tell them as a last resort.

4. After the correct pairs of words have been established, ask the class to "brainstorm" other words that have the same vowel sounds as some of the pairs; three or four words is enough per pair. For example, *hat*, *black*, *flag*, and *crab* contain the same sound as the *cat/back* pair.

5. Ask the students to write a couple of sentences, where each sentence is based on one of the word clusters. Each sentence should contain at least three words which have the same vowel sound. The two examples below are based respectively on the *might/cry* and *few/use* word pairs:

   > The shy boy cried last night.
   > The girl must use her new blue shoes.

   The sentences are, of course, a little artificial, but the students find them fun to do and they provide valuable pronunciation practice. It is important to check that the sentences are correct because they will be used as the basis of step 6.

6. Ask each student to read one sentence, which the others should copy in their notebooks. The sentences may not be read more than twice. Ask the students to come to the front, one by one, and write the sentences they dictated on the board in clear handwriting so that the others can check their work. When they have checked each sentence, read it to them in a lively, animated but natural way to reinforce the correct pronunciation.

7. To finish off, ask the students to choose a sentence or part of a sentence they would like to be able to say with zest and real confidence. As they practice, move behind the students and become the "human computer" again as described in step 1, but this time working on stress and intonation, the music of the language.

Author's Note

This recipe contains a medley of ideas I first came into contact with at the School for International Training in Brattleboro, Vermont. The idea of the "human computer" comes from Charles Curran's "Community Language Learning."

Loren McGrail

§

TELEPHONE ENCOUNTER

Unit III / AUDITORY ACTIVITIES / Level: Intermediate and above / Time: 30 minutes plus 30 minutes if step 3 is done in class

Language Function(s): Exchanging and comparing personal information, creative writing

Materials: Copies of the list of questions on page 35

Before Class

Copy the list of questions on page 35.

In Class

1. Draw a large telephone on the board. Ask the students to think about telephones for a moment or two. Have a quick show of hands to test whether their basic feelings about telephones are positive, negative, or mixed.

2. Divide the class into pairs. Distribute the copies of the questions on page 35. Tell the students they have about 20 minutes to discuss them. They should avoid answering in one or two words. Stress that the activity is intended to give them the opportunity to speak freely. Encourage them to open up, ask questions and develop the conversation as fully as possible. As they begin their discussions, move around the class, helping the students as necessary. That's all there is to it! You'll be amazed at how much the students will have to talk about.

3. Follow the activity up by assigning a creative writing exercise on one of the following topics:

    A phone call I'll never forget
    The telephone—a necessary evil?
    An old telephone recounts some conversations it has been involved in

The length of the assignment and the question of whether it should be homework or classwork will depend on the time available and the level of the class.

Christopher Sion

§

DISCUSS THE FOLLOWING POINTS WITH YOUR PARTNER

- When the phone rings, how do you feel?
- Who do you speak to regularly on the phone?
- Who do you look forward to speaking to?
- Who do you dread speaking to?
- Which phone numbers do you know by heart?
- Can you recall some recent occasions in which you looked up a number in a telephone directory?
- Do you ever "take the phone off the hook?" When? Why? How do you feel about doing this?
- How do you feel when you are connected with an automatic answering device?
- Can you recall some recent telephone conversations (personal and professional)?
- Can you recall any messages you took or were given recently?
- How do you prepare yourself for an important phone call?
- How do you feel when you have to speak English on the phone? What problems do you encounter specifically?
- Do you have a phone at home? How many phones do you have? Which rooms are they in?
- Who usually answers the phone in your home?
- What is the best time and what is the worst time to call you?
- Have you ever had any sinister, unusual, or amusing calls?

FAST FORWARD LISTENING

Language Function(s): Listening comprehension, reading for gist

Materials: Cassette recording of a reading passage, copies of the text, cassette recorder with counter

Before Class

Find or make a recording of an interesting reading passage at the level of your class. The passage should not be longer than about 25 lines, except in the case of very advanced classes. Number the lines of the text in multiples of five and make copies of it for the class.

In Class

1. Distribute the copies of the passage to the class. Allow a couple of minutes for students to read it. Tell the class that the important thing is only to have a general grasp of the contents of the passage. Do not read through the passage with the class in great detail explaining every word and phrase. This step is to practice "skim reading" or "reading for gist."

2. Spin the cassette to a random point, note the counter reading (or set it on zero) so you can find the place again easily, and play a section of the recording of the passage. About one or two lines should be enough. Tell the class that their task is to say which line(s) they have heard. Spin the cassette back once or twice if necessary. Encourage the students to read out whole lines, or refer to key phrases in the lines rather than shouting out a cacophony of numbers.

3. Continue by winding the cassette back or spinning it forward and playing short sections as described in step 2. Be sure to keep an eye on the counter. Once the activity has developed a good rhythm, start reducing the length of the sections you play until they are down to a handful of words. For variety, you can let a few students take turns at operating the recorder, but be sure to stop while class interest is still high.

4. Finish off the activity by playing the whole recording from start to finish.

Author's Note

This technique can bring even the dullest text to life. The students find it exciting and it has the effect of waking everybody up. It leads the students to listen carefully, recognize the words on the cassette aurally, visualize their written form, and scan the text to find them.

Allan Ryding

§

TUNE IN TO A STORY

Unit III / AUDITORY ACTIVITIES / Level: Intermediate / Time: 20 minutes

Language Function(s): Making associations of words and music

Materials: None

Before Class

Prepare an interesting, varied story containing lots of detail. In fact almost any story or incident will do, such is the power of the mind at making associations.

In Class

1. To warm up the class, divide the students into pairs and ask them to discuss what their favorite pieces of music are. Do they have a favorite piece of folk, jazz, classical music, pop, rock, film music, etc? Two or three minutes should be ample for this step.

2. Ask the class, still working in pairs, if they associate any piece of music with a particular story or an incident from their lives. If so, they should tell their partner the story.

3. Now inform the class that you are going to tell them a story (this being the story you prepared before class). If the students hear anything that reminds them of a piece of music, they should interrupt you and should briefly sing or hum the music in question. If the students are too inhibited to sing or hum, they may prefer to explain the association in a couple of sentences. Be sure to keep the pace brisk.

4. Tell the story slowly, letting the students interrupt you as described in step 3. For example, if your story began: "When I was downtown yesterday morning a lady wearing a green sweater asked me the way to the White House . . .," students might interrupt you with "Downtown," "Early One Morning," "Greensleeves," or "The Star-Spangled Banner."

5. Retell the story, this time without interruptions. The associations will probably remain, which will be an effective means of recalling the content of the story and reinforcing the relevant language.

Author's Note

This activity is most suitable for closely integrated classes in which the students don't feel uncomfortable about singing in company. It is also only suitable in cultures where it is not socially taboo to interrupt the teacher.

Martin Rinvolucri

§

E THER WAITER

Unit III / AUDITORY ACTIVITIES / Level: Low intermediate / Time: 10 minutes

Language Function(s): Identifying and practicing sounds

Materials: A cassette recorder and recording of the song(s) are useful, but not necessary

Before Class

Check that you know the words and melody of the song "Show Me the Way to Go Home."

In Class

1. Tell the class that you heard an incredible song the other night, although it doesn't seem to make much sense. Some of the words from the song were *waiter, ether, Tire Dan,* and *goat.* Ask the students what they think the song could possibly be about.

2. Continue in the same vein, being sure to keep a straight face. Tell the class that you liked the song so much you tried to write down all the words, even those you couldn't understand. Perhaps the class can help you. The song went like this:

   > Shome ether waiter go home
   > I'm Tire Dan I wanna goat abed

   Write this text on the board.

3. The next step is to tell the students that the tune is so nice you would like to sing it with them, even if the meaning is not clear. Use a cassette recording for support if you can.

4. Turn to the class in pretended amazement. What's that you say? Did I hear you correctly? Did you say "Show me the way to go home. I'm tired and I want to go to bed?"

5. Write the song on the board correctly and then sing it again the same way as the first time, in other words, so that it really flows naturally. Invite the whole class to join in. This amply makes the point that you needn't pause for five seconds between words even if you are low intermediate.

Mike Levy

Publisher's Note

Another example which is ideal for this approach is the well-known song "Mairzy Doats."

§

UNIT IV

WORKING WITH WORDS

"The word *fascism* has no meaning except in so far as it signifies something undesirable."

George Orwell

READING COMPREHENSION

Language Function(s): Asking and answering questions

Materials: Monolingual English dictionaries, copies of a reading passage, copies of the students' questions

Before Class

First lesson: Select and copy a fairly demanding reading passage for the level you are teaching. The passage should be between one and two pages long and should preferably fall into four or five clear sections. Give each section a letter or number for easy identification.

Second Lesson: Check that the students' questions are in acceptable English and that they are legible. Make copies of the questions.

In Class

1. Divide the class into four or five groups and give each student a copy of the passage you selected. Each group should be provided with at least one copy of a monolingual English dictionary. Tell the class that each group is going to be responsible for one section of the text. Establish which groups are going to work on which sections.

2. Tell the students that their task is to prepare about 10 comprehension questions on their particular sections of the passage. Explain that you will collect their questions and will make copies of them for use in the next lesson. Ask the students to write clearly so that their questions can be read easily by their classmates. If students are not sure what you mean by "comprehension questions," explain that comprehension questions are intended to test whether a passage has been understood. Give them a couple of examples. Once the students have started work, circulate, helping with any difficulties as necessary.

3. Collect the questions for use at the next lesson. (See "Before Class, Second Lesson.")

4. At the next lesson, divide the class into the same groups once again. Distribute the questions in such a way that each group is given a set of questions written by one of the other groups. Their task is to answer the questions. This means that each group of students will be answering questions about a section of the passage that they did not work on before. They can work individually, in pairs, or as groups. For convenience, it is preferable for the students to write on loose sheets of paper, not in their notebooks.

5. Collect the answers when the students have finished. Give the answers to the groups that set the questions at the first lesson. Their task is now to correct the answers as if they were examiners.

6. When the answers have been corrected, they should be returned to the students who wrote them. The answerers may challenge the markers' decisions and the markers should try to justify themselves. This step should lead to some lively interaction. Be sure not to let the exchanges get out of control.

7. Finish the lesson with a general discussion of the logic of comprehension questions and the value of comprehension tests. To what extent does being able to answer a question correctly really mean that a text has been understood? Encourage the students to back up what they say by requiring them to cite examples of specific questions.

Author's Note

This activity is particularly suitable for students preparing for examinations which involve "traditional" reading comprehension papers, as it helps the students appreciate how an examiner's mind works.

Pat Charalambides

§

Language Function(s): Developing an awareness of register and the importance of context when doing translations

Materials: Copies of the text and the word lists (see "Before Class"), bilingual dictionaries, typing correction fluid

This activity is only suitable for linguistically homogenous classes.

Before Class

1. Select or create an English text appropriate to the level, needs, and interests of the class. It should be about one page long.

2. Using typing correction fluid, delete 10 to 20 words from the text you have selected. Wherever possible, these should be words which are open to several interpretations when taken out of context. Words such as *basic, common, park, book, space, expansion, area*, or *foundation* are ideal.

3. Write the deleted words in random order on a separate sheet of paper as a hand-out. The words should be spread over the entire sheet.

4. Prepare a second hand-out of the deleted words with translations into the students' first language. The translations should be appropriate to the word's context in the passage. Jumble the translations so that they do not follow the same sequence as the words on the first hand-out.

5. Make copies of the two hand-outs and the text.

In Class

1. Divide the class into two groups. Give copies of the English word list to one group and copies of the translations to the other. Tell each group to look for as many acceptable translations for the words on their lists as they can think of collectively. The first group will be translating into the students' own language, the second from that language into English.

They should take varying contexts into account as much as possible. For example, *draw* could mean to draw a picture, to pull (a horse drawing a cart), or to feel consoled (to draw comfort). What are acceptable translations of these different meanings? The translations should be written next to, or around, each word on the lists. Dictionaries may be used.

2. Tell the students to find a partner from the other group to work with. Their task is to cross-check their translations by matching the words on the two word lists. Partners' translations which had not been thought of should be added to the students' own lists.

3. Arrange a "plenary session" in which the translations and alternative contexts can be discussed, verified, or rejected.

4. Tell the students to predict the content of the text the English words were taken from (which, of course, they still haven't seen). Tell them to work in pairs and then report their ideas to the whole class.

5. Distribute the expurgated version of the text and tell the students to complete it using the list of English words. They should consider all the possible alternatives and accept or reject them on the basis of appropriateness and context.

6. Finish the lesson by telling the class what the words in the text actually were.

Martin Worth

§

IV-3 TV SPONSORS

Language Function(s): Persuading, describing and imagining, asking and answering questions

Materials: List of one day's television programs taken from an English language newspaper or TV guide

Before Class

Cut the list of one day's television programs from the newspaper or TV guide. Select the four most important channels and cut out these four channels' programs separately. (If one program is printed on the back of another, make a copy of one side of the page.) If four channels are not available, use the programs from more than one day so that you have four alternative programs.

In Class

1. Divide the class into five groups. One group is to play the part of the Committee of Sponsors. Each of the remaining groups is allocated one of the four main TV channels. Call them groups 1, 2, 3, and 4. Explain to the whole class that the sponsors are trying to select a set of three programs to broadcast all over the world by satellite. The channel that wins the sponsorship will receive $1,000,000.

2. Give groups 1, 2, 3, and 4 a copy of the TV channel they have been allocated. Tell the four groups that their task is to sell three of their programs to the Committee of Sponsors. The four groups should describe (or invent) what their programs are about. They should find convincing reasons why the committee should support their proposals. The stakes are high so they should be as persuasive as possible. The sponsors should meanwhile establish the criteria by which they intend to judge the programs and should work out some questions to interview the four groups about their choices. Encourage the sponsors to devise critical questions as this will force the other groups to argue their cases vigorously.

3. Tell the four groups to present their selections to the committee. When one group is presenting, the others should listen carefully and draw attention to any weak points in the arguments. A certain amount of heckling is acceptable, but don't let the activity get out of control.

4. The sponsors retire to consider their verdict. This again involves the language of persuasion among the different committee members. While the committee members are conferring, the other students may be told to discuss the merits of their opponents' programs so that they are not sitting idly.

5. The sponsors return and deliver their verdict. The winners will receive their check as soon as the programs are broadcast!

René Bosewitz

§

Language Function(s): Asking and answering questions, practicing adjectives

Materials: Small cards

Before Class

Make a list of about twelve occupations; for example: dentist, window cleaner, pilot, slaughterhouse worker, trapper, model, missionary, hairdresser, teacher, professional tennis player, actor/actress, and carpenter. Be sure to include some occupations with negative associations, such as slaughterhouse worker and trapper, so that the negative adjectives generated in step 1 can be used. This is important because so many books only deal with the more pleasant side of life. The majority of the occupations you select should be known by the students, but be prepared to answer any questions that arise. Write one occupation clearly on each card.

In Class

1. Warm up the class by asking the students to think of as many adjectives as they can that can be applied to people; for example: hard, kind, considerate, stubborn, mean, affectionate, attractive, moody, caring, and so on. Write them on the board. The adjectives generated will naturally depend on the level of the class. Check that everybody understands the vocabulary.

2. Divide the class into pairs and give each pair one of the cards. Tell the pairs to select about ten of the adjectives on the board that most precisely describe the qualities a person needs to do the job written on their cards. For example, for the job of missionary, students may decide that a missionary needs to be kind, considerate, and caring, but with a hard, stubborn streak, which will be useful in dealing with authorities in developing countries, and so on.

3. Tell the pairs to imagine taking on the identity of the occupation they have on their cards and to introduce themselves in that identity. Thus, the pair which has "model" may introduce themselves by saying: "We're flirty, sexy, and dumb—although only at first sight. In fact we're very sensitive and always wanted to do something creative." Note any stereotypes that arise (see step 5).

4. As the pairs introduce themselves, the rest of the class should ask questions to try and establish what the occupation is. The questions may only be answered "Yes" or "No." Examples of such questions are: "Do you work indoors?" "Do you provide a useful service to the community?"

5. You will almost certainly find that some students revert to stereotypes such as the absent-minded professor, sadistic dentist, and superficial model. If you are interested in the topic, this provides you with the ideal opportunity to start a discussion on the nature of prejudice. As a lead-in to this subject, ask the students to make a list of a few well-known stereotypes. Then ask the students to think of people they actually know from these different walks of life. How do the people compare with the stereotypes?

Claudia Kniep

Editor's Note

A useful reference book if you are interested in step 5 is: Gordon W. Allport, *The Nature of Prejudice* (Addison-Wesley).

§

IV-5 ATEGORIES

Language Function(s): Categorizing vocabulary

Materials: Postcard-size cards

Before Class

Write one category together with five or six words related to it on each of the cards. You need enough cards for every student to have one. If the class is very big, you should prepare one card for every two students. Try to choose categories and words that your students are likely to know. Here are some examples:

Things that you listen to
- music
- radio
- teacher
- friend
- gossip

Things that are red
- roses
- cheeks
- cherries
- apples
- blood

Words beginning with ph
- philosophy
- phrase
- photograph
- physics
- phone

Two-word verbs
- call up
- look like
- do over
- get up
- run into

In Class

1. Give each student one of the cards. Tell the students they have five minutes to prepare. Their task will then be to take turns at describing their words to the rest of the class. The descriptions should be as quick and as brief as possible. No gestures are allowed.

2. When the five-minute preparation time is over, the students describe their words as outlined in step 1. The rest of the class should try to guess what the words are as quickly as they can. They should then try to establish what the category is. If you want to stir up the more competitive side, you can divide the class into teams or appoint an umpire to supervise the activity. Personally, I prefer the whole group approach because that way the student is only competing against himself or herself.

Author's Note

This activity was inspired by The School for International Training in Brattleboro, Vermont.

Loren McGrail

Editor's Note

"Category Game" on page 69 also has ideas on using categories.

§

BLACK BAGS

**Unit IV / WORKING WITH WORDS / Level: High intermediate and above /
Time: 20–30 minutes**

Language Function(s): Describing, speculating, comparing

Materials: Several opaque bags (cloth, paper, or plastic), unusual objects such as baby toys, small electrical plug with a wire to attach to the outlet, part of a domestic appliance, small piece of equipment used in rock climbing or fishing, and so on

Before Class

Put the unusual objects into the bags, one object per bag. Close the bags securely.

In Class

1. Divide the class into groups of three or four and give each group one of the bags. Tell the groups to agree on a description of the object they can feel in the bag. Emphasize that it is a *description* that is wanted. It is not important for them to be able to name the objects at this stage. Encourage the students to make notes, in other words, to write the description briefly on pieces of paper.

2. Pair each student with someone from another group. Tell the students their task is to take turns to describe the object they felt so that their partners can draw it. The students should use their written descriptions as a starting point to which they then add more detail.

3. Inevitably the students will want to know what the objects are. Let the students say what they think the objects are and then open the bags one by one and compare the contents with the drawings.

4. Conclude by naming the objects and, if necessary, explaining their functions.

Dermot Murphy

§

 DISCOVERY WORDS

Language Function(s): Vocabulary acquisition

Materials: A large picture containing many details, such as a landscape or street scene. Copies of pages from an English dictionary such as Webster's *New World Dictionary*, the *Random House Dictionary* (College Edition), the *Oxford Advanced Learner's Dictionary* or Longman's *Dictionary of Contemporary English*.

Before Class

Copy some double pages of an English dictionary so that you have one double page for each student. You can give everybody copies of the same page or use different pages, but be sure to check that the pages contain a fair variety of words that may reasonably be applied to the picture.

In Class

1. Display the picture prominently at the front of the class and then give out the copies of the dictionary pages. Ask the students to look at their pages and select up to five unfamiliar words which they feel they could use when talking about the picture. Tell the students to share these initial associations in pairs or small groups. The students can explain the associations if they wish. Be sure to accept all their ideas.

2. Now ask the students, working individually, to write sentences using their newly discovered words. The sentences can be in whatever context the students wish. They may be, but need not be, related to the picture. Allow about 15 minutes for this phase. Advise and correct as necessary.

3. Divide the class into pairs and tell the students to discuss and compare their sentences. If some pairs finish before others, let the students change partners, several times if necessary, so that everyone is kept active but without the slow ones being pressured.

4. When the whole class is ready, ask each student to read one sentence aloud to the class. Tell the students to listen for similarities between the readers' sentences and their own. This ensures a high degree of listening involvement.

Author's Note

It is a good idea to repeat this activity several times during a course.

Mike Lavery

§

PHRASAL T-SHIRTS: A MARKETING EXERCISE IV-8

Language Function(s): Reviewing two- and three-word verbs, presenting information

Materials: Simple line drawings of T-shirt outlines are useful, although not essential

Before Class

Copy the T-shirt outlines if you plan to use them.

This activity assumes you have already covered an exercise on phrasal verbs (two- or three-word verbs) in a recent lesson and are now ready to practice them.

In Class

1. Begin by asking for some examples of slogans written on T-shirts. Briefly discuss what these slogans mean. Does anybody have a T-shirt with a slogan on it? Is anyone wearing one today?

2. Ask the students to recall a phrasal verb exercise you recently did. Which of the phrasal verbs can they remember? Prompt the class as necessary and write the phrasal verbs on the board as the students think of them. Ideally you need 20 to 30 examples. Allow the students to refer back to the exercise if they wish. Check that the meanings are clear.

3. Distribute the copies of the T-shirt outlines or tell the students to draw simple T-shirt outlines for themselves. Then tell the class to use some of the phrasal verbs on the board in slogans and to write them on the T-shirts. The more examples the better. Encourage the class to be as imaginative as possible. The students can work alone or with partners. Ask the students to read their best examples to the whole class.

4. Reorganize the class into groups of three or four. Tell the students to pool their slogans and to discuss and explain them to each other. The students should add any new slogans they happen to think of. This step should not take more than about five minutes.

5. Tell the groups that they should imagine that they are T-shirt manufacturers. Each group should give itself a name; for example, "International T-Shirt Corporation" or "Close Fit Company." The groups should then decide on next year's range of T-shirts. Which sizes and colors and in which fabrics are they going to produce? At which prices? Most important, which slogans are they going to print? Which slogans will they combine with which colors and sizes? Which slogans do they expect will sell best? What are the different target groups for the different ranges of T-shirts? What are the most appropriate slogans for these different target groups? What quantities do they plan to produce?

6. Ask the class to reassemble and let the groups report back to the whole class. Suggest that the groups split up the role of spokesperson so that everybody gets the chance to speak. For instance, one group member can report on the colors, another on the prices, a third on the reasons for selecting the slogans, and so on. Allow a couple of minutes for the groups to prepare this as necessary.

Author's Note

As described above, this activity limits itself to phrasal verbs. It goes without saying, however, that any other vocabulary can be consolidated in exactly the same way.

Christopher Sion

§

DO-IT-YOURSELF CLOZE TEST

Language Function(s): Practicing vocabulary

Materials: Pages from newspapers

Before Class

Decide on a vocabulary area you want to focus on, for example, verbs, prepositions, two-word verbs, words with Latin or Anglo-Saxon roots, or mixed metaphors. Check that the newspaper does indeed contain a fair variety of articles with words that belong in the vocabulary area you have selected.

In Class

1. Divide the class into small groups. Tell the students which vocabulary area you want to focus on (see "Before Class") and then distribute the pages from the newspaper so that each group has one page. Tell the students to look for an interesting article with lots of examples of the vocabulary area you selected.

2. Tell the groups to read through their articles and to black out the words which belong to the vocabulary area so that they cannot be read. The articles may be shortened if necessary. The students should keep a separate written record of the words they have blacked out. It is a good idea to number these words and the blacked out spaces for convenience. In this way the students write their own cloze tests. Any words which are not clear should be looked up in a dictionary.

3. Now tell the students to exchange their tests with those of the other pairs or groups. The students should try to fill in the words which have been deleted. When this task has been completed, the students should get together with the makers of the tests they have just done and discuss the answers. How appropriate are the words? Do any new words change the meaning, register, tone, and so on?

Author's Note

This activity is a good lead-in or follow-up to Unit 12 of Saxon Menné's *Writing for Effect* (Oxford University Press).

Marjorie Baudains

Publisher's Note

The *Dictionary of Reading* published by the International Reading Association says that the term *cloze* was coined by W. Taylor in 1953 "to reflect the gestalt principle of 'closure,' the ability to complete an incomplete stimulus."

§

CLEANLINESS: A SWISS PASTIME

Language Function(s): Practicing vocabulary in context

Materials: Typing correction fluid, copies of the "whited out" version of the text and the list of missing words

Before Class

1. Select a text according to the level of your class. The text may be from whatever source you wish, but it should obviously be something the class is likely to find stimulating. A sample text, "Cleanliness: A Swiss Pastime," can be found on the following page.

2. Using typing correction fluid, "white out" a selection of words that you want the students to concentrate on. Do not omit the same word more than once. Number the words and the blanks as this will speed up the process of checking.

3. List the words in alphabetical order and in their simplest form; that is to say, nouns should be in the singular, verbs in the infinitive, and so on.

4. Copy the "whited out" version of the text and the alphabetical list of missing words.

In Class

Distribute the copies of the text and of the list of words. Tell the students to fill in the blanks using each word once only. They should modify the words according to the structure of the sentences the words have been deleted from. Allow the students to work individually, in pairs, or in small groups. Encourage them to use dictionaries (preferably monolingual ones) if they are available. (The solution to the sample text appears below.)

Author's Note

This activity is useful for work on grammatical and semantic awareness. It can be used both for revision and for breaking new lexical ground. Select your text according to your purposes.

Margrit Wehrli

Editor's Note

A good idea when using exercises of this sort is to make a more complex version (with more words missing) for the better students. It may also be possible to make several versions corresponding to the varying language needs of the different language groups one would have in a multilingual class.

Solution

1. invented	9. dropped	17. judging
2. imagine	10. throw	18. ruin
3. used	11. ritual	19. blankets
4. litter	12. praise	20. exposed
5. dead	13. invention	21. unfortunately
6. flower	14. runs	22. seriously
7. wrapper	15. assessing	23. repeated
8. addressing	16. gossip	

§

Cleanliness: A Swiss Pastime

The Swiss fascination with cleanliness has led to habits which may explain Swiss eccentricity to visitors to their country. Some years ago the Swiss (1)_____ a street vacuum cleaner, which does not, as you might (2)_____, rid the streets of (3)_____ tram tickets, bottle tops, beer cans, or chocolate wrappings. As a matter of fact, such (4)_____ is never to be found there in the first place. The machine is for (5)_____ leaves, (6)_____ petals, and dust. Just try to get rid of your chewing gum (7)_____ in a Swiss town by carelessly throwing it away in the street and you will find a helpful Swiss picking it up, (8)_____ you with the following words: "Excuse me, I think you've (9)_____ something." Just you dare (10)_____ it away a second time!

Let me now turn to another, yearly (11)_____, the one in (12)_____ of spring-cleaning. No (13)_____ is required for this activity as it serves a double purpose: first to get everybody's house super clean; secondly to establish the cleanest household of the year. Every street (14)_____ its private competition, with neighbors (15)_____ each other and finally passing on the winner's name by word of mouth, or by what is more commonly known plainly as (16)_____. Here are the criteria for (17)_____: Has all the living room furniture been thoroughly aired in the garden, preferably under trees so as not to (18)_____ the finish of the wood or the color of the fabric? Have cushions, eiderdowns, pillows, (19)_____, and bedspreads been (20)_____ to the sun and beaten at regular intervals?

If you ever visit Switzerland in spring you will have the chance to see how the Swiss live and to imagine what their homes look like. (21)_____, you will not be invited to anybody's house at this time of year. But do not think summer would be any better, because by then everybody would be (22)_____ worried that their houses were no longer up to standard, although the spring-cleaning ritual is (23)_____ on a smaller scale every Friday. Go mountain-climbing instead!

Missing vocabulary
address; assess
blanket
dead; drop
expose
flower
gossip
imagine; invent; invention
judge
litter
praise
repeat; ritual; ruin; run
serious
throw
unfortunate; use
wrapper

UNIT V

READING AND WRITING

"Examinations are formidable even to the best prepared, for the greatest fool can ask more than the wisest man can answer."

Charles Colson

Unit V / READING AND WRITING / Level: Variable, intermediate in the case of the story included here / Time: 30 minutes

Language Function(s): Expressing agreement and disagreement

Materials: Copies of the stories

Before Class

1. Write and then duplicate two versions of the same story. The versions should begin in the same way and then gradually deviate from each other. Try to disguise the discrepancies as subtly as you can so that a sharp student does not see through the exercise too soon.

2. Organize the copies of the two stories so that they can be distributed without drawing attention to their differences. It is probably best to mix them together alternately so that it is easy to distribute more or less the same number of copies of each version (see: In Class, step 1).

In Class

1. Distribute the two stories without drawing attention to the fact that they are not identical. Be sure to hand out approximately the same number of each version.

2. Ask the students to read their stories and memorize the contents. Move round the class, helping as necessary, and then take the stories back.

3. Ask one of the students to tell his or her story. The other students should listen to it carefully and make sure it is correct. Disagreement will soon result, with different students supporting or rejecting the stories being told. Let other students take over the function of storyteller after a while so that the one student does not monopolize the activity.

4. Distribute the stories again, still without admitting that they are different. Some students will probably have the version they originally had, others will have the alternative version. This increases the confusion and therefore forces students to read the texts with particular care.

5. After a few minutes, confess. Give out more copies so that every student has both versions. Finish with a discussion of the activity with particular reference to the feelings of indignation and frustration which arose.

Author's Note

Two variations of this activity are as follows:
  a. Distribute copies of the same version of the story to all the students except one. This person should be one of the best students, preferably someone with a strong personality. He or she should be given the alternative version of the story and should be asked to relate it to the group. Be sure to organize the activity without drawing attention to the fact that there is a trick somewhere.
  b. Organize the stories alternately (A-B-A-B) so that they can easily be distributed systematically round the class. This variation is easiest to set up when the students are sitting in a horseshoe formation. After the stories have been read and collected the students should be paired with a partner (the student they are sitting next to) who will have read the other version. Tell the pairs to reconstruct the story.

Randal Holme

§

Cathy and the House

At first Cathy liked her new house. It was large, spacious, and had a garden you could get lost in. The only thing that worried her was the house next door. There was something strange about it. Even when a strong wind was blowing, it seemed to be very still. Cathy used to tell her brother the house was covered in glass, so the wind never touched it. One day they decided to explore the house to see if the glass was there. Cathy was nervous and her brother went in front of her. Suddenly her brother stopped. He was pushing against a wall that Cathy could not see. "You silly boy," she said. Her brother laughed and they both crept up to the edge of the garden. They saw nobody so they ran across the grass.

"Can you feel the wind?" Cathy asked. Her brother had to admit that he could not.

They reached the front door. Cathy crept along the wall to look in at the windows. The house was dark and empty. She came back to her brother. The air felt heavy. They could not move. They pushed the door. They felt something pull them through the open door. They could not do anything. They were lost in the darkness, held by it like by a huge hand.

Cathy and the House

At first Cathy liked her new house. It was large, spacious, and had a garden you could get lost in. The only thing that worried her was the house next door. There was something strange about it. When a strong wind was blowing, it seemed to move like a tree. The house creaked in the wind. Cathy used to tell her brother the house was trying to say something, although it was covered in glass. This meant that no one could understand it. One day they decided to explore the house to see if the glass really was there. Cathy was not nervous so she went in front of her brother. Suddenly her brother stopped. He was pushing against a wall that Cathy could not see. "You silly boy," she said. Her brother was afraid and started crying quietly as they both crept up to the edge of the garden. "I think I can see somebody!" he cried as they ran across the grass.

"It's only the wind. Can you feel the wind?" Cathy asked. Her brother had to admit that he could not. He felt much better now.

They reached the house. Cathy crept along the wall to look in at the windows. The house looked warm and friendly. She came back to her brother. The air smelled sweet. They did not want to move. They gently pushed open the back door. They felt something pull them through the open door into the kitchen. They could not do anything except move into the darkness. The old man held out a huge hand. "Tea will be ready in a moment," he said.

READING, WRITING, AND RECALL

Language Function(s): Making associations

Materials: Large pad of paper (a "flipchart" or newsprint pad is ideal), thick felt-tipped pen, thumbtacks or adhesive tape

Before Class

Think of some suitable discussion topics relevant to the interest and level of your class. Good examples are: "Women in Modern Society," "Mankind and Machines," "No More than Two Children per Couple" or "Space Is the Future."

In Class

1. Explain that you are going to write a suggestion for a possible discussion topic on the flipchart. (A flipchart is better than a chalkboard since the individual pages can be torn off as they fill up with vocabulary and can be conveniently fixed to the wall.) The moment the title appears, the students are to say any words and ideas they associate with it out loud.

2. Write the discussion topic on the flipchart. The associated words will come forth at varying rhythms from the students. All the words, phrases, quotations, abbreviations, images, and so on should be written on the flipchart as the students call them out. Help students who are looking for elusive new vocabulary or trying to recall words only recently learned. Occasional pauses will probably occur, but with patience and a little unobtrusive prompting the tempo will soon pick up again.

3. When the students can find no further associations, ask the class to look through the ideas you have collected on the flipchart. Which words or phrases can be grouped together? Tell the class to debate which expressions belong in sets. It is a good idea to identify these groups of words with a number, letter, or symbol. There is frequently a miscellaneous group of words with no apparent associations at all. Here

is a selection from the topic "Women in Modern Society":

A	B	C
secretary	house	equality
salary	children	discrimination
machine	cleaning	marriage
slave	cooking	Women's Lib

You should copy each set of words onto a large sheet of paper from the flipchart. Then fix the sheets of paper to the wall.

4. Ask each member of the class to choose the set of words he or she would most like to speak about or which he or she feels most strongly about. Then divide the class into groups according to which sets of words the students have chosen. Each group is to collaborate in writing a paragraph containing all the words included in its set of words. Move around the room checking and providing help as necessary.

5. A spokesperson for each group reads out that group's paragraph. The paragraphs should be discussed, criticized, and corrected. The other students can call on the groups to explain and justify what they have written.

6. This is an optional step which may be used to review the material. Collect the paragraphs and type them so that they can be distributed at a subsequent class as a document for analysis and further discussion. The sets of words can also be typed and distributed to provide students with a written record of the basis of the lesson.

Roy Sprenger

§

STORIES BY ASSOCIATION

**Unit V / READING AND WRITING / Level: Intermediate to advanced /
Time: Two 20–30 minute sessions**

Language Function(s): Making associations, narrating

Materials: None

In Class

1. Elicit any six words from the class, for example: *sun, leather, woman, mother, office, dog.* Write the words on the board.

2. Divide the class into six groups. Each group should work on one of the six words. No two groups should be assigned the same word. Tell the groups to concentrate on their respective words and to think of as many associations as they can with their words. The associations need not be direct. In fact, the more spontaneous and imaginative the associations, the better. Ask the groups to delegate students to come and write their lists on the board. From the set of words listed in step 1, the groups might produce sets of words such as the following:

SUN	LEATHER	WOMAN
moon, stars, planets, hot, astronomy, telescope, lens, bright	plastic, silk, cloth, material, rubber, cowhide, whip, imitation	man, animal, child, attractive ugly, sexy, kind

MOTHER	OFFICE	DOG
father, warm, family, pregnant, baby, busy, unappreciated	typewriter, stapler, desk, calculator, chair, boss, prison	cat, mouse, rat, kennel, bark, bite, friend, bone

3. Tell the students to copy down all six lists of words. Check that they understand the meanings of any new words. Then ask the students to write a story *using at least one word from each of the six sets of words.* You may wish to assign this for homework and offer a small prize for the story including the most words from the six lists.

4. At the second session, once you have collected and corrected the stories, ask the students to reassemble in the same groups they were in before. Each group should nominate a spokesperson to read its story to the whole class. As the stories are read out, the class should pay careful attention in listening for the words from the six lists as they occur.

Bryan Robinson

Editor's Note

The initial brainstorming phase serves as a valuable creative stimulus. Many teachers probably feel that attempts at creative writing with their classes are doomed to failure, when all that is really needed is a simple warm-up activity to spark off the students' imaginations.

§

V-4 READING INTO A ROLE

Language Function(s): Asking and answering questions

Materials: Copies of the texts

Before Class

Select or write about five short texts with a common underlying theme. The texts should largely be written in the first person singular. The level of the material should be slightly below the comprehension level of the students, and the content should be sufficiently vague to allow a wide degree of interpretation. Several examples are included on page 57. Copy several sets of the texts.

In Class

1. Divide your class into groups of three to five students. Give each group one set of texts, a different text to each student in each group. Ask the students to read their texts but not to show the texts to each other. Help the students with vocabulary, pronunciation, and so on as necessary, while allowing them to work as independently as possible.

2. Ask one student in each group to read his or her text aloud to the rest of the group. The other members then ask the reader questions related to the text. The reader must answer these questions in character, in other words, as if he or she were the *I*-character in the text. This necessitates going beyond the scope of the texts. The reader has to draw on his or her own imagination to fill in the role.

3. Repeat with the other students now taking turns to read their texts, be questioned by the groups, and reply as described in step 2.

4. Finish with a whole class discussion of the activity. How did the students feel in their roles? Was there another role from another text they would rather have been assigned?

Author's Notes

1. The reading stage has two functions: it serves as a communicative exercise in reading aloud and as an input to role-playing. It is vital that the texts should not fill out the roles with too much detail, as this deprives the readers of the chance to develop their own ideas.
2. The questioning stage enables the readers to construct their roles gradually, with help and encouragement from the groups. In my experience, the groups are naturally cooperative and supportive to the readers.

John Morgan

§

When I saw my friend I could not speak. For two or three minutes we just stood and looked at each other. Finally I spoke, but the words came out all wrong. I knew what I wanted to say, but I couldn't say it.

My father and I never talked. Sometimes he said something, but we never talked to each other. Perhaps other people's fathers are like that too. I don't know. Perhaps if we *had* talked, things would be different now.

I write a lot of letters. Sometimes I write three or four in one day. I write to everybody—to my family, to my friends, to the newspapers. Perhaps some day I shall write letters to myself.

I tried to telephone today. I stood in the phone box for half an hour before I picked up the receiver and dialed. I let it ring twice. Then I put the phone down. I tried again after ten minutes. I heard it ring ten or twelve times, but no one answered. I was glad, really.

When I started to speak, everyone laughed. When I started again, they began to look uncomfortable. I spoke for about half a minute, and I could see that they were embarrassed. People looked at their feet, or out of the window. Some of them made excuses and left. Then my mother told me to go into the kitchen and help my sister.

V-5 ILENT DIALOGUES

Language Function(s): Asking and answering questions, expressing opinions

Materials: A large chalkboard and lots of chalk, copies of a reading passage (see: Before Class)

Before Class

Select and then copy a short reading passage (maximum one page) at the appropriate level for your class. The passage should be on a topic likely to interest the majority of the students, and should require them to express their opinions.

In Class

1. Divide the board into two halves, one for questions, the other for opinions. Distribute the copies of the reading passage and ask the students to read it silently. Tell the students to write any questions they have about any aspect of the text in the question section of the board. They should state any opinions they have relating to the content of the text in the opinion section. Tell the students that if they can, they should also write the answers to their classmates' questions on the board. Moreover, they should feel free to write up counter opinions if they disagree with the statements on the opinion side of the board. All of this is to be done in complete silence.

2. When the students no longer have contributions to write, or when you sense the silent dialogues have gone on long enough, divide the class into small groups and tell them to discuss the passage orally.

3. Finish the activity with a short discussion of the activity. How did the students feel about what they were required to do? Has anybody changed his or her opinion?

Author's Notes

I wish to acknowledge that I learned this technique from a teacher trainee at Pilgrims Language Courses (Canterbury, England) in 1978.

The advantages of the technique are:

a. You do not have to spend time writing comprehension questions.
b. The silence allows time for thought unaffected by an addressee; it allows time for reference back to the text; and it allows time for careful peer teaching.
c. The silence builds up the need to talk within the students.

Mario Rinvolucri

§

# DEAR BOSS

Unit V / READING AND WRITING / Level: Intermediate / Time: 60 minutes

Language Function(s): Expressing preferences, voicing criticism, making suggestions

Materials: None

In Class

1. Divide the class into small groups. Ask the students to think about their working day, the environment they work in, and the people they work with. What are they dissatisfied with? Tell the groups to discuss what could be improved. (If your students are not business people but are still in school or university, adapt the instructions to an educational setting.)

2. The students should now work individually. Their task is to write a letter to whomever they are responsible, such as manager, headmistress, dean of university faculty, and so on. The letter should detail the improvements the students would like to have implemented and should begin:

"Dear Boss,
If I were you, I'd . . ."

Circulate as the students write, checking their English and providing help as necessary.

3. When everyone has finished writing, tell the students to read their letters to the whole class. The class should listen carefully and then decide whether the complaints are justified and whether the suggested improvements are practical. In my experience the students often focus on genuine problems in their working lives.

Author's Note

Mini-Recipe 1 on page 111 provides a good lead-in to this activity.

Martin Worth

§

V-7 COMPOSITION BY CARDS

Language Function(s): Writing sentences, narrating

Materials: Small cards, one per student

Before Class

Select a number of words you want to review with the class. Base your selection on words which you are sure your students will be able to combine in sentences. Write one word clearly on each of the cards. You need one card per student.

In Class

1. Give one card to each student. Then ask each student to make one sentence using the word on the card. Check that they all understand the words on their cards.

2. Ask one student to read out his or her word. The others should try to combine this word with the word on their own cards in a sentence. For example, Anita reads out her word: *director.* Magda has *shoot,* and makes the sentence: "Sometimes I would like to shoot the director." Ramon's word is *cold,* so he makes the sentence: "The director doesn't like the winter because it's cold."

3. Divide the students into groups of three or four. Tell the groups to make as many different combinations of their words as they can. Minor transformations of the words are permissible; for instance, verbs may be changed into the past tense form, plurals of nouns may be used, and adjectives may be in the comparative or superlative forms. Imagine a group with the words *shoot, dislike, communist, teacher.* They may produce sentences such as: "The communists shot the teacher because they disliked her," "The teacher was a communist who disliked shooting animals as a hobby," or "The teacher disliked living in a communist country so much that he shot himself." The more combinations the students make and the more inventive they are, the better.

4. Bring the whole class together again. Tell the groups to appoint a spokesperson to read their best sentences to the class. Then tell the class you want to write a story combining all the words. Encourage as much discussion as possible about the form the story should take. Once the story line is clear, write the final version on the board and allow time for the students to write it down if they wish to.

Author's Note

This idea was inspired by a workshop on creative writing at Pilgrims Language Courses Summer School in Canterbury, England.

Bryan Robinson

§

UNIT VI

GAMES AND SIMULATIONS

"If we taught our children to speak they'd never learn."

William Hull

THE HUMAN FLOW CHART

Unit VI / GAMES AND SIMULATIONS / Level: High intermediate to advanced / Time: 45–60 minutes

Language Function(s): Suggesting, agreeing and disagreeing, expressing opinions, presenting information

Materials: Small cards, thick felt pens, copies of the complete list of steps on page 63. You need a room which allows the students to stand up and move around freely.

Before Class

Analyze a suitable marketing action plan into individual steps as in the example on page 63. Write each step on a card and shuffle the cards well. Make copies of the complete list of steps.

In Class

1. Give each student one of the cards you have prepared (see: Before Class). If there are more cards than students, keep the additional cards for later in the activity. If there are fewer cards than students, let some students share.

2. Have the students stand up and arrange themselves in a physical line on the basis of the steps written on their cards. This line represents the chronological order of the steps on the flow chart. (A little lively background music will loosen up the atmosphere and encourage even the most reluctant students to leave their seats and join in the activity.) Tell the students they are to read each other's cards and decide in which order they should stand. Some steps clearly follow others. For example, "Research the market" obviously comes before "Test the prototype," which in turn comes before "Start production." Other steps such as "Forecast domestic sales" and "Forecast export sales" may occur simultaneously.

3. If it proves difficult to determine a feasible sequence, tell the students to stop moving around for a while and to hold a discussion to determine how the steps in the sequence need to be rearranged. If you have not given out all the cards yet, this is the moment to do so. Once a logical sequence has been established, the students may again try to arrange themselves in the sequence if they wish. When this step has been completed, instruct the students to return to their seats.

4. Have the students brainstorm the various departments to be found in a large corporation. A sample list is on page 63. Write their suggestions on the board.

5. Divide the class into small groups and distribute the copies of the complete list of steps to be sequenced. Ask the groups to categorize the steps on the lists according to the departments that they consider would be responsible for each step in a typical corporation. For example, the Research and Development Department will be responsible for testing the prototype. Distribute blank cards and felt pens. Tell the students to write the name of the departments at the top of the cards and list the departments' responsibilities below these headings. The groups classifications can refer to real or imaginary departments in real or imaginary organizations. A lot will depend on the students' background and experience. For instance, you may expect different classifications if you are using the activity in an MBA course or an in-house corporate training program.

6. Have the groups take turns to report their analyses to the whole class. These reports should take the form of short presentations. Each group should be given the choice of appointing a spokesperson to do the presentation or sharing this function between the group members.

Marketing Action Plan Steps

Research market data (requirements, etc)
Analyze competitors' products (if any)
Determine product specifications
Develop prototype
Test physical product on market
Develop brand image
Test brand image on market
Test physical product and brand image together on market
Forecast domestic sales
Research export market
Forecast export sales
Estimate investment and manufacturing costs
Forecast total sales (including break-even point and profit growth)
Review whole project and approve
Start production and launch product

Departments

– Production
– Export
– Advertising
– Research and Development
– Sales and Marketing
– Market Research
– Board of Directors
– Financial Control

Author's Note

The supplied lists of marketing steps and responsible departments are only models. Real-life situations may well include other steps such as purchasing machinery, advertising, training the sales force, and purchasing raw materials. The organization of departments will vary from one corporation to another. Sales and Marketing, for example, may be split in some corporations. Refer students to their own experience wherever possible.

Martin Worth

Editor's Note

The activity as described here is obviously only suitable for students with a business background. However, *"The Human Flow Chart"* can be adapted to any activity that involves a series of discrete steps that must (or should for efficiency) be done in discrete steps. Other examples are buying a new car, building a house, and making the arrangements (domestic, professional, and medical) for a new baby in the family.

§

TUDENT MIMES

Language Function(s): Writing dialogues, speculating

Materials: Small pieces of paper or card, cassette recorder, cassette recordings of lively music; you also need a classroom which allows the students to move around easily and in which you can arrange a small open area for the mimes

Before Class

Write a particular location such as *HOTEL, RESTAURANT, HOME, STATION* or *STREET* on each of the cards. It is preferable to have a different location on every card, although it is not essential. Organize the seating arrangement in the classroom so that you have an open space for the students to perform in.

In Class

1. To warm up the students, start with any simple physical loosening up activity. I ask the students to begin by waving a finger, then a whole hand, then the hand and arm below the elbow, then from the shoulder, then the other arm, then a leg, then the other leg, and so on, until the whole body has been loosened up. Gently coax any reluctant students into participation. This step is essential in helping students overcome their inhibitions. Once it gets going, it usually results in plenty of laughter.

2. Tell the students to stand up and move freely around the open area you have arranged. Play some lively background music on a cassette recorder to create a suitably relaxed atmosphere. After a few minutes, stop the music and divide the class into groups of four according to where they are standing when the music stops.

3. Give each group one of the small cards with a location on it (see: Before Class). Tell the class that two students in each group should write a short dialogue that takes place in the location specified on their card. The other two students in each of the groups will later be asked to act out the dialogue in mime. The mimers remain involved throughout the writing phase as they have the right to veto anything they regard as impossible to mime. Tell the class that it is vitally important that the students in any particular

group do not discuss their cards or their dialogues with the other groups at this stage (see: step 5). Move around the classroom, helping as necessary.

4. As preparation for step 5, write a number of locations on the board. This list should include the locations you have written on the students' cards as well as other locations. Do not indicate which are which. The purpose is to pre-teach the vocabulary the students will need in step 5, particularly the correct use of prepositions and articles in collocations such as "in a hotel," "in a restaurant," "at home," "at the station," or "in the street" (see: step 5a).

5. Ask one pair of mimers to come to the open area and act out their mime to the rest of the class. Once they have finished, the other students should make suggestions concerning the following points:

   a. WHERE does the mimed scene take place?

   b. WHO is speaking to WHOM?

   c. WHAT are the characters meant to be saying to each other?

   d. ANYTHING ELSE.

6. After the students have speculated about the mime as described in step 5, the writers of the dialogue should read it aloud. This provides the rest of the class with listening comprehension with a purpose, namely the confirmation, or otherwise, of what they imagined was being mimed. During this phase, be sure to draw attention to any phonological, grammatical, or lexical errors that arise in the dialogues.

7. Ask the other groups to take turns at presenting their mimes and reading their dialogues as described above.

Author's Note

I learned the loosening up technique from a teacher at the TESOL Portugal Conference, in Rio Tinto, Oporto in 1984.

David Cranmer

§

VI-3 WORK EXPANDS

Unit VI / GAMES AND SIMULATIONS / Level: High intermediate / Time: 20–30 minutes

Language Function(s): Speculating, combining words into sentences

Materials: Small pieces of paper; you require a room in which the students can move around freely

Before Class

Parkinson's Law that "work expands to fill the time available" can be expressed in many ways.

Three possibilities are:

Work expands to fill the time available. (7 words)
Work will always expand to fill the time which is available for its completion. (14 words)
It is invariably true that work expands to fill the time available for its completion. (15 words)

Prepare a version of Parkinson's Law relative to the level of your class. Ideally the version you choose should contain as many words as there are students in your class. In a large class you may have to let pairs of students share some of the words. When you have decided on your version, write it down clearly—one word per piece of paper.

In Class

1. Give each student one of the pieces of paper, which means that each student will have one word from the version of Parkinson's Law you prepared. Make sure that the students understand their words.

2. Tell the students to stand up and arrange themselves into a "living sentence" on the basis of the words on their pieces of paper. Do not tell them that you have cut up an actual sentence. The students can either simply show each other their words or, which is more challenging, tell them to memorize the words then say them to the class. This second option demands clear pronunciation and close listening. This step should take about five minutes.

3. Tell the class to return to their seats and list all the words they have seen or heard (i.e., the words from the pieces of paper). The students may work alone, in pairs, or in small groups—let them decide for themselves. Then proceed as follows:

   Possibility A: The students *did not* find the version of Parkinson's Law you prepared when they were doing step 2. Explain that all the words together make up one sentence. The students should try and find that sentence.

   Possibility B: The students *did* find the version of Parkinson's Law you prepared when they were doing step 2. Tell the students to try and make other sentences using only the words on the pieces of paper. They need not use all the words.

4. Ask the students to report back to the whole class. What sentences did they find? If the students have still not discovered that the words can be combined to make up the version of Parkinson's Law you have been using, write it on the board for them.

5. Finish with a general discussion of Parkinson's Law. If interest permits, assign a homework composition on "Work expands to fill the time available."

Author's Note

For further information see C. Northcote Parkinson, *Parkinson's Law* (Penguin).

Gerry Kenny

§

OUTER SPACE SIMULATION

Unit VI / GAMES AND SIMULATIONS / Level: High intermediate / Time: 60–90 minutes

Language Function(s): Describing and imagining, comparing ideas

Materials: Ideally you need three rooms

Please note that the activity requires a class of at least 15 students.

In Class

1. Divide the class into three groups. Tell the students to imagine that each group represents the population of a different planet from outer space. Ask the groups to create a description of their respective planets in as much detail as possible. The following points should be included: the name of the planet, a physical description of the environment, a physical description of the inhabitants, the character of the inhabitants, a taboo, a current problem the planet is facing.

2. If you are fortunate enough to have three rooms available, tell each group to go to one room. If you only have one room at your disposal, tell the groups to work in different areas of the room. Explain that you would like the groups to think of the rooms (or areas) they are going to work in as their planets. Go around from group to group, providing help as necessary.

3. When the groups have developed fairly full descriptions of their planets, ask one person from each planet to visit both the other two planets. Tell the visitors their task is to observe and bring back as much information as possible about the other planets. However, the visitors are not allowed to communicate in any way with the beings of the planets they visit. They should restrict themselves to observation.

4. After a while, tell the inhabitants of the three planets to discuss the current problem the planet is facing (see step 1). If they wish, they may refer to the other points mentioned in step 1, either explicitly or implicitly. Tell the inhabitants that they should not attempt to communicate with the visitors.

5. When the visits are finished, ask the visitors to return to their planets and report what they have observed.

6. Go to each group in turn and ask the students to imagine that the intergalactic government has decided that two of the three planets must be depopulated. Everybody must go to live together on one planet. The three groups should each decide which of the planets is the most suitable on the basis of the visitors' reports.

7. The students reassemble as one class. Tell the students to hold a meeting with the following objectives:

   a. Each group should inform the others about which planet they chose and why.

   b. Any misunderstandings that may have arisen should be clarified. (For instance, a visitor may have misinterpreted an aspect of what he or she observed.)

   c. The whole class should try to reach agreement about which planet they all should live on.

8. Finish the simulation with a general discussion. What did the students particularly like and dislike about the activity? Which language points did they handle successfully? Which other points still require work?

Richard Baudains

§

ROUP DYNAMIC QUIZ

**Unit VI / GAMES AND SIMULATIONS / Level: High intermediate to advanced /
Time: 60–90 minutes**

Language Function(s): Asking and answering questions

Materials: None

Before Class

Decide how you are going to divide the class. You should group the students in two teams of equal strength with regard to language level and general knowledge. You should also take the students' personalities into account. Don't put all the extroverts in one team and all the introverts in the other.

In Class

1. Divide the class into two teams as described in the "Before Class" section. Tell the teams their task is to formulate 10 detailed quiz questions which require comprehensive answers of several sentences. Questions such as: "When was the Russian Revolution?" (Answer: 1917) are not satisfactory. A suitable question and answer on the same subject are:

   Question: What famous event took place in Russia in 1917? Who were the main protagonists and what were some of the consequences?

Answer: The Russian Revolution began in 1917. Trotsky, Lenin, and Stalin were important personalities. It started in Leningrad. Later Lenin died and Trotsky was murdered by Stalin. Stalin become dictator of the Soviet Union.

Go around the class, helping as necessary, while the teams prepare their questions.

2. The students reassemble as one class. One member of both teams should put a question to the other team so that the teams work in parallel. This way the teams can discuss the answers to their respective questions simultaneously, without wasting precious time in class. Team members should take turns to ask and answer the questions so that nobody monopolizes the talking.

Author's Note

The teacher should play the role of umpire. I recommend you score as follows: Award three points for an answer which is both factually and linguistically correct and is sufficiently detailed. Award one or two points for answers which are less comprehensive or are only partially factually correct. Award up to two minus points for mistakes in grammar and idiom. Answers which are factually incorrect score no points.

René Bosewitz

§

CATEGORY GAME

**Unit VI / GAMES AND SIMULATIONS / Level: Elementary to intermediate /
Time: 15–20 minutes plus 20 minutes if you do step 5**

Language Function(s): Asking and answering questions, speculating, categorizing vocabulary

Materials: None

Before Class

Prepare a few examples of categories such as those listed in step 4.

In Class

1. Explain the idea of categories by giving a few simple examples: What do Maria's eyes, your shirt, the sky, jeans, a bruise, and the sea have in common? (They're all blue.)

2. Ask one or two students to come to the front and face the class. Explain the rule clearly that these students may not look at the board. Then write one category on the board and ask the class to call out examples of things that belong to this category. For instance, typical items belonging to the category "Things that open and close" are: doors, bars, mouths, bank accounts, art exhibitions, boxes, and so on. The students who are calling out examples should not say what the category is. The examples should be written on the board.

3. After a few minutes, erase the category and tell the students at the front that they may now look at the list of items. Their task is to establish what the category is. They can ask their classmates questions and make suggestions as to what other items they think belong to the mystery category. Help with a few examples of your own if the students at the front get stuck, but do not prompt to the point where

you destroy the students' pleasure at "cracking the category."

4. Repeat the game with other students at the front and other categories. Some examples you'll enjoy using are:

   things that come in pairs
   things you can (or cannot) buy
   things you keep in the fridge
   things that scare people
   things that have numbers
   things that get better with age
   things you associate with students
   things you find in an infant's room
   things that have holes
   things that are invisible

5. If interest permits, brainstorm all the different categories the students can think of. Encourage the students to be as imaginative as they like, although they should restrict themselves to categories for which examples are easy to find. Write the examples on the board. Then divide the class into pairs or small groups. Tell the students they have 10 minutes to make lists of as many items belonging to two or three of these categories as they can.

6. A spokesperson for each group reads out one of their lists of items.

Author's Note

I learned this activity from an American TV quiz show, "The $10,000 Pyramid."

Michele Meyer

Editor's Note

Another recipe, called simply "Categories," approaches the subject from a different point of view and may be found on page 44.

§

VI-7 THIS IS MY ELBOW

Language Function(s): Reviewing vocabulary (body parts), intensive listening

Materials: None

In Class

1. To warm the class up, draw a simple outline of a person on the board. Write words such as *hand, ear, finger, thumb, leg* next to these body parts. Elicit as many examples you can from the class. Write the words elicited on the appropriate part of the drawing.

2. Ask one student to come to the front of the class. Together demonstrate a couple of examples such as the following:

   Touch your elbow and say: "This is my nose." Explain that the student should reply by touching his or her nose and saying: "This is my elbow." It is now the student's turn to contribute. If the student indicates his or her head while saying: "This is my foot," you should reply by touching your own foot as you say: "This is my head." Make sure that everyone is quite clear about what is required.

3. Divide the class into pairs and tell the students to practice as many similar examples as they can. Encourage the students to think of odd combinations. Just because they have used a word once does not mean they need no longer practice it. The more repetition the better!

Author's Note

Although this exercise is rather bizarre, it requires intense concentration and coordination and is great fun. It goes without saying that you should only use it for review purposes. If you try to introduce the vocabulary in this way you will only create confusion.

Sid Phipps

§

IFTEEN

Unit VI / GAMES AND SIMULATIONS / Level: Elementary / Time: 15–20 minutes

Language Function(s): Practicing numbers, calculating

Materials: Dice, three per student group

Before Class

Secure lots of dice. Considering that for a class of 20 students working in 5 groups of 4 you need 15 dice, it is advisable to ask the students to help you by bringing their own if you have a large class.

In Class

1. Draw large +, −, ×, and ÷ signs on the board. Then spend a few minutes checking through the language of calculating with the class, for example: 2 plus 2 is 4; 10 minus 7 is 3; 5 times 5 is 25; 16 divided by 2 is 8. Elicit as much of this language as you can from the students.

2. Explain the rules of the game as set out at the end of this recipe. Supply enough examples so that the aim of the game is quite clear when the students commence playing.

3. Divide the class into groups of about three to five students. Have one student in each group act as a secretary whose function it is to keep score. (The secretaries may participate in the game themselves if they wish to.) Give each group three dice. Wish the students good luck and tell them to start playing.

The Rules

a. The players take turns to throw three dice. In each turn, the dice should be thrown altogether in one throw, not individually.

b. Players must try to get as near as possible to 15 (or less) in each turn.

c. Points are calculated as follows: Players may not simply add up the points showing on all three dice they have thrown. Combinations of the four basic calculating operations (addition, subtraction, multiplication, and division) must be used in making the calculations. Each number thrown must be used once (and may not be used more than once).

$$\boxed{5} \times \boxed{6} + \boxed{3} = 15 \qquad \boxed{5} \times \boxed{2} \times \boxed{1} = 15$$

$$\boxed{1} \times \boxed{4} \times \boxed{2} = 8 \qquad \boxed{6} + \boxed{5} + \boxed{6} = 7$$

d. Each player keeps a tally of the numbers resulting from each calculation he or she has made. The overall aim of the game is to reach 100 or above. In other words, the first player to reach (or pass) 100 is the winner. When the game has been won, the players in each group are free to decide to stop, continue playing in order to establish second and third places, or start a new round as they wish.

Peter Schimkus

§

VI-9   THE ROBERTS FAMILY PHOTOGRAPH

Unit VI / GAMES AND SIMULATIONS / Level: Intermediate / Time: 30 minutes plus 30 minutes for step 6

Language Function(s): Socializing, exchanging information

Materials: Small cards; you need a room in which the students can move around freely; if possible, a camera and film

Before Class

Copy the information about the Roberts family (see page 74) onto the cards. The activity as presented here is intended for sets of 12 students. However, this number can be reduced or increased by modifying the number of family members. If you change the composition of the family at all, be sure to alter the Identity Cards carefully so that the information they contain is accurate and consistent.

In Class

1. Tell the students to imagine that they belong to the Roberts family. The family members have not met for a very long time. In fact, their last meeting dates from so long ago that they do not recognize each other at first sight! Today is a special occasion and the whole family has come together once again.

2. Continuing outlining the scenario by saying that a family photograph of all the people present will be taken for this special occasion. Before the photograph can be taken the members of the family must establish who's who.

3. Give each student one of the Identity Cards on page 74. Stress that these cards MUST NOT be shown to the other students. Explain that the Roberts family members should try to find each other's identities by socializing and exchanging information about themselves. For example, Jim will begin a conversation with another student by saying something like: "Hello, there! My name's Jim. I love playing football. Do you by any chance collect butterflies? I'm looking for my brother and he collects butterflies."

4. Invite the class to stand up and move around the room. Tell the students to talk in twos and threes at first, as if they were at a cocktail party. It is not so effective for the whole class to huddle together in one clump at the beginning of this stage of the activity. Move around the students monitoring their language, offering help and correction as necessary, and perhaps making notes on language points you want to deal with afterwards.

5. When the family relationships have been clarified, tell the students to take up their positions for the photograph. Ask each person to introduce himself or herself briefly. If you are lucky enough to have a camera you can actually take a photograph of the group.

6. An optional additional task is to tell the students to write a page about themselves in the identities they had as members of the Roberts family. Suitable titles for this page would be "What happened to me since I last saw my family" or "The story of my life." This task may be done in class or assigned as homework.

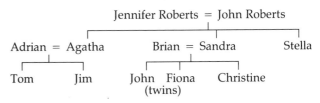

The Roberts Family

72

Author's Note

I wish to acknowledge that I learned this activity from Dave Allan.

Ray Janssens

Editor's Note

Even though the situation of not recognizing family members is artificial in that husbands and wives could not realistically be expected not to know each other, this has never proved a problem when I have done the activity with a class. In my experience the students slip into the roles with no difficulty. Sometimes on discovering a long lost brother or sister I've actually had students throw their arms around each other in a friendly embrace!

§

Identity Cards

STELLA

1. You are an art collector.
2. You're divorced.
3. One of your nieces is studying art.

JIM

1. Your brother collects butterflies.
2. You are a professional football player.
3. Your father plays golf.

CHRISTINE

1. Your father is a sailor.
2. Your aunt has a fine collection of paintings.
3. Your brother and sister are twins.

SANDRA

1. You're married to a sailor.
2. Your father is a businessman.
3. You have three children.

TOM

1. You play the drums.
2. Your cousin is a nurse.
3. You collect butterflies.

JOHN

1. You're a carpenter.
2. Your twin sister is a nurse.
3. Your grandfather is a businessman.

ADRIAN

1. You are a businessman.
2. You play golf.
3. You have two sons.

BRIAN

1. Your mother-in-law is a teacher.
2. Your son is a carpenter.
3. One of your nephews is very good at sports.

FIONA

1. Your sister is an art student.
2. Your grandmother is a teacher.
3. You're a nurse.

JENNIFER ROBERTS

1. You are a teacher.
2. Your granddaughter lives in Paris.
3. Your younger daughter is divorced and has no children.

JOHN ROBERTS

1. You have three daughters.
2. Your elder daughter has two sons.
3. Her husband is a businessman like you.

AGATHA

1. You have two younger sisters.
2. You have two nieces and a nephew.
3. Your father is a businessman.

COPS AND ROBBERS

**Unit VI / GAMES AND SIMULATIONS / Level: Intermediate to advanced /
Time: 40–60 minutes**

Language Function(s): Compiling, checking, and sharing information; making and evaluating decisions; persuading

Materials: Copies of the instructions and map on page 76, small cards (preferably of different colors)

Before Class

Prepare copies of the instructions and map on page 76. Copy the 15 items of information from the information file on page 77 separately onto small cards, one item per card. (The class will be working in groups of four to six students. You need one set of 15 cards for each group.) The cards in each set should be shuffled together so that they are not in any particular order. For your convenience when it comes to collecting the cards after the activity, it is a good idea to use a different color for each set of cards.

In Class

1. Divide the class into small groups. Give each student a copy of the instructions and map (see: Before Class.) Allow a few minutes for the class to read the instructions so that the point of the activity is perfectly clear from the outset.

2. Give each group one set of instructions (see: Before Class.) Distribute two or three cards to each student. The cards should not be shown to the other members of the group. Moreover, the information may only by shared *orally* within the groups. This rule makes the activity more communicative and all the students are obliged to participate.

3. When the students have read their instructions and the information on their cards, tell them to discuss whether the man should be arrested. If possible, the groups should reach unanimous decisions. Explain that there is no one right answer to the problem.

4. Ask a spokesperson from each group to report the group's decision to the whole class.

5. Finish the activity with an evaluation session in which the groups discuss and compare the following points:

    a. How were the decisions made? What criteria were used?

    b. How was the exchange of information organized?

    c. Are Bonilla and Vargas one and the same person? Is there enough information to make a rational decision?

    d. Did the students express themselves accurately in the group work?

    e. Did the students work well together in the groups? Were the students sensitive to their classmates' needs? Was the information adequately repeated? Did everybody listen to each other? Was the turn-taking in the discussion fairly distributed among the group members? Did anybody dominate the discussion to the disadvantage of the others? Did anybody emerge as a "democratic leader"?

    Dermot Murphy

§

Instructions

For this game you should imagine you are a U.S. police detective on duty in Laredo on the Texas-Mexico border.

It is noon on 16 January. A man who might be a foreign criminal has been stopped at the border. His passport says he is Antonio Bonilla, but he looks like Antonio Vargas who is a well-known gangster.

Each of the students in your group has information which will permit you to establish together whether this man is a criminal and what his movements have been in the last two weeks. You have 20 minutes to do this.

You can order arrest for crimes such as murder or armed robbery committed in another state, but not for the theft of a car (unless this was done in Texas).

Should you arrest this man?

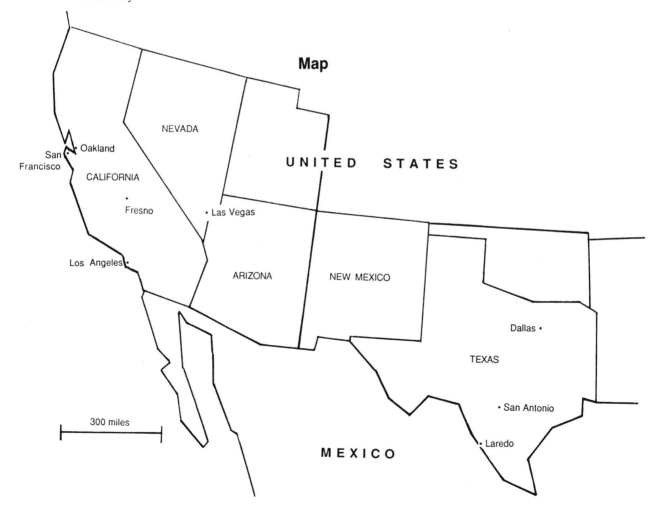

Map

Information File

A man called Bonilla was among suspects arrested in San Francisco following a large theft from airport warehouses. He was held at police headquarters on the nights of 5 and 6 January and all day of 6 January.

A man called Bonilla was released by San Francisco police on 7 January.

A man called A. Vargas registered at a hotel in Fresno, California, on the night of 11 January.

Vargas spent 3 January in Dallas, Texas.

You have confirmation that Bonilla spent the night of 15 January in a hotel in San Antonio, Texas, 300 miles south of Dallas and 150 miles from the Mexican border.

Vargas was stopped just outside San Antonio at 9 a.m. this morning for speeding.

Vargas was thought to have been seen in Los Angeles, California, on 6 January.

A clerk in a Los Angeles car rental agency has recognized a snapshot of Vargas. The register shows he rented a car from January 10–13. The same clerk saw him on both days.

Bonilla crossed the border at Laredo early on 3 January in a car.

You have a report that A. Vargas was in Dallas yesterday, 15 January.

A man called Vargas was seen in Las Vegas, Nevada, on 4 January and then again on 14 January.

A Las Vegas, Nevada, bank was robbed by three men on the afternoon of 12 January. A bank clerk was killed. One of the men, Carlos Melgosa, has been arrested.

A. Vargas was in a hotel in Oakland, California, on the night of 10 January. On the morning of 11 January he had a car accident in Oakland and the car was in a garage for repairs for the next 48 hours.

Vargas has used other names: Alejandro, Aurelio, with the surnames Villa, Bonilla, and Valle.

On average twenty cars are stolen and driven away every day in San Antonio.

VI-11 FUN WITH HEADLINES

Language Function(s): Writing newspaper headlines, agreeing and disagreeing

Materials: Thick felt pens, interesting pictures from newspapers, adhesive tape, simple joke prize (see step 5), scissors, a room with space for the students to move around freely, pieces of paper

Before Class

Cut some pictures from newspapers. You need one picture for every two students. Pictures with some action in them are more suitable than portraits.

In Class

1. Divide the class into two teams. Ask each team to appoint a captain and have the other students in the teams work in pairs. Have one group of three if you have an odd number of students. The captains should not be members of a pair.

2. Give each pair one of the newspaper pictures, a piece of paper, and a felt pen. Tell the pairs their task is to write a newspaper headline for their pictures. The headlines should be written clearly in large letters on separate pieces of paper, not on the pictures. While the headlines should be appropriate to the pictures, it should not be too obvious which pictures and headlines go together. For example, don't write "Man dives into swimming pool" for a picture showing a man diving into a swimming pool. Less direct headlines such as "Wet feet" or "Head first" are what is required.

3. When the pairs have finished writing, the headlines and pictures should be handed to the captains. Ask the two captains to exchange the headlines and pictures. The captains should then position themselves on opposite sides of the room and should stick the pictures on the wall with tape so that they can be seen clearly.

4. Tell the class that when you give the "Go!" signal, the captains should show their teams the headlines. The teams should then try to match the headlines with the pictures. This will probably cause considerable disagreement. When the teams decide which headline belongs with which picture, the captains should tape the headlines under the pictures they are thought to refer to. The winning team is that which correctly completes the matching in the shortest possible time.

5. Ask the teams to leave their seats and go to their respective captains. Give the signal to start and let the teams do the activity as outlined in step 4. If you wish, award a simple joke prize such as a cardboard badge for the "Award Winning News Team of the Year" or " Gold Medal" to the winning team.

Susan Cattell and Ben Duncan

Editor's Note

If your class is bigger than about 20 students, it is advisable to work with three or even four teams, or the game may get out of control. If you have fewer than 10 students, give the pairs two or more pictures so there is enough material to make the game interesting.

§

Language Function(s): Narrating, indirect speech, expressing conditional statements, speculating

Materials: None

Before Class

Prepare the story carefully. Make sure you can explain any new vocabulary easily.

In Class

1. Tell the class that you are going to tell them a story and that you will ask them to act out the various situations being narrated as the action unfolds. This will sometimes be in small groups and sometimes with the whole class. Encourage the students to assume and change roles liberally from scene to scene.

2. Tell the students the following story in whatever way you like, but without giving all the facts at once. Explain new vocabulary briefly as it arises. Some suggestions for interspersing the role allocation with the narrative are included in italics at the beginning. Continue in the later stages of the story by allocating roles and drawing the students' attention to language points in the same way.) Encourage the class to be as imaginative as possible and allow the students to incorporate their own ideas into the story.

Uncle Joe's Last Fling

Uncle Joe lives with relatives and is beginning to get on in years. One day he announced he is going to take a walk in the park. He wants to buy a newspaper and have a drink in his favorite bar. He will be back in time for lunch at one o'clock.

(Valerie, would you play the part of Uncle Joe's sister, Fred you be the brother-in-law and Igor, you be Uncle Joe in this scene.)

One o'clock comes and goes. Soon it is 2, 3, 4 p.m. and no sign at all of Uncle Joe.

(Louisa and Stefan, you be the sister and brother-in-law this time, please. Why not get on the phone and call other friends and family to ask if they have seen Uncle Joe. Please try to use sentences such as: "He said he was going to the park," "He said he would be back for lunch," "I hope nothing has happened to him," "If he's not back by 6 o'clock I'm going to call the police" and so on.)

6:30 p.m. By now several friends and relatives have gathered at Uncle Joe's apartment. Has he gone mad, has he been mugged or kidnapped, has he developed amnesia and forgotten the way home? Might he be stuck in the elevator? Or is he still in the bar?

7:00 p.m. The frantic family call the police, who as always are cautious about following up missing persons cases.

(Once again, tell the students to use indirect speech to explain what Uncle Joe said he was going to do. Tell them to persuade the police to take the matter seriously in view of Uncle Joe's age and the fact that he has never been late or missing before.)

About 48 hours later a report comes in from a resort in California where the police claim to have seen an old gentleman answering Uncle Joe's description having dinner with a mysterious woman in a five star hotel.

(The parts to be role-played here are the California police calling the police in Uncle Joe's home town, the local police contacting the family and the family's reactions: "But that couldn't be Uncle Joe!" "Uncle Joe would never do that!" and so on.)

(At this point, reveal the true facts of the case to the class, who will now be thoroughly intrigued by the story.)

In fact, Uncle Joe never even got to the park. Before buying his newspaper, curiosity led him to play the horses at a betting shop he had often passed on his walks. He placed a $10 bet on a rank outsider which then won the race at odds of about 100 to 1. Uncle Joe took his winnings and went for a quiet weekend on Coney Island. He just wanted "to get away from it all" for a while.

Uncle Joe now returns home, looking very well indeed! He doesn't realize that a gentleman answering to his description has been seen wining and dining in California. His friends and relations are very suspicious of his story about Coney Island. So are the police.

(From this point on, the students themselves can be given a free hand in furnishing further details!)

3. Follow up the classwork by assigning "Uncle Joe's Last Fling" as a written homework. The students can choose whether they want to write in narrative or dialogue form and can have a free hand in altering or embellishing the story.

Mike Perry

Editor's Note

The narrative should be "fed" to the class as follows: a. Tell a line or two of the story. b. Allocate the roles for the part of the story you have just told. c. Comment on the language. d. Have the students act out the roles. e. Tell the next part of the story.

§

Teacher Development: Practical Reflections on Teaching

"What is happening when nothing is happening in a group?"

John Heider

A-1 HE ICEBERG

Appendix A: / TEACHER DEVELOPMENT / Time: 20–30 minutes

Focus: Classroom awareness, particularly of hidden factors in the learning process

Materials: Copies of the two icebergs (pages 83 and 84)

Comment

As described here, this activity is intended for teacher trainers to use with students following programs in order to become teachers of English as a foreign language. However, the content of "The Iceberg" may also be worked through outside the classroom situation, either individually or by discussing the issues raised with fellow students or professional colleagues.

Before Class

Make copies of the two icebergs on pages 83 and 84.

In Class

1. Distribute copies of the blank iceberg on page 83. Ask the students to consider the relationship between the iceberg and the learning process. What can be seen clearly? What is more difficult to see? It is advisable not to give too much input at this stage in case you block the students' spontaneous answers. Some examples may be found on page 84. Tell the students to write their thoughts on the appropriate parts of the iceberg hand-outs. Visible factors should be above the surface and semi-visibles below the water line.

2. Divide the class into pairs and give the students about five minutes to discuss their ideas with their partners.

3. Draw a large iceberg outline on the board. Ask each pair to contribute one or two important points to be written around the iceberg. Once this "class iceberg" has been completed, distribute copies of page 84 for comparison.

4. Finish with a general discussion of ways in which teachers can take the factors referred to in "The Iceberg" into account in everyday teaching situations. How can teachers sensitize themselves to what is going on in their classes? What can they do to facilitate more effective teaching?

Mike Lavery

Editor's Note

Obviously this is only a beginning. It is not suggested that definitive answers to these questions can be expected in a short discussion session.

§

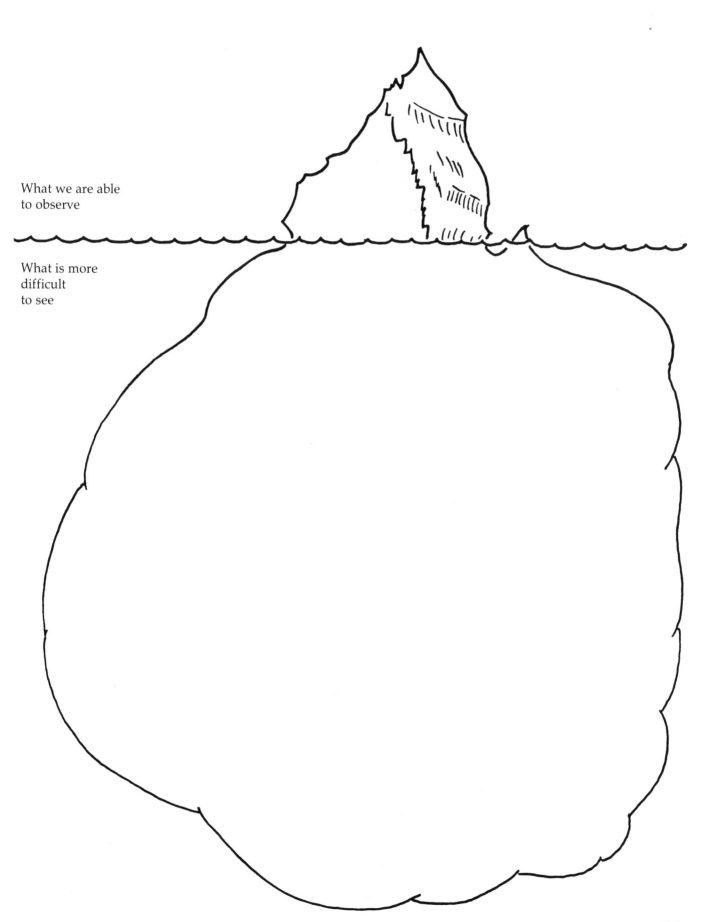

What we are able
to observe

What is more
difficult
to see

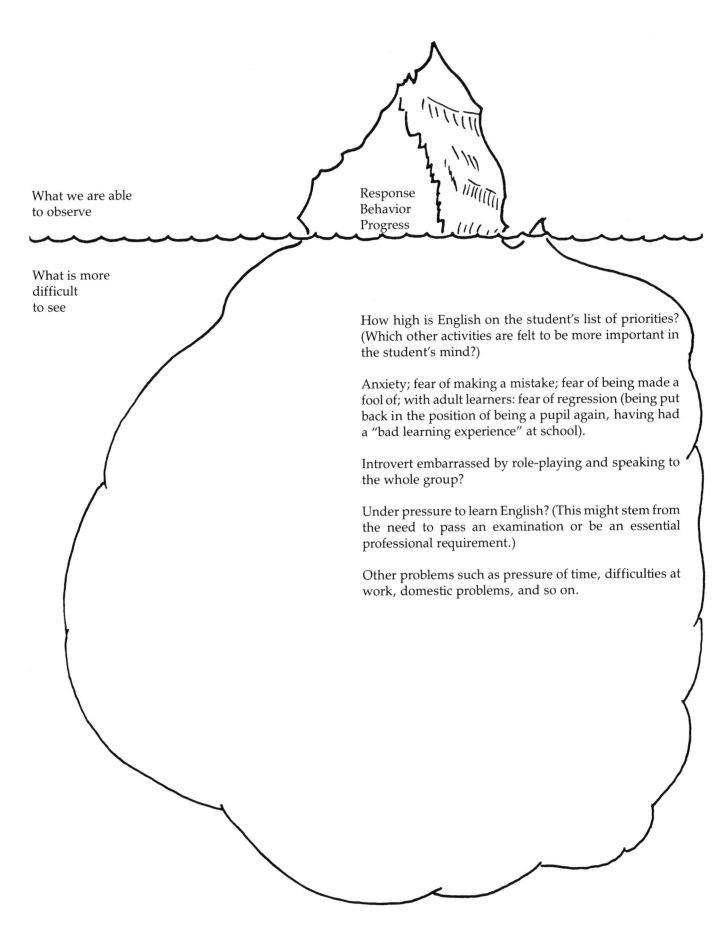

What we are able
to observe

Response
Behavior
Progress

What is more
difficult
to see

How high is English on the student's list of priorities?
(Which other activities are felt to be more important in
the student's mind?)

Anxiety; fear of making a mistake; fear of being made a
fool of; with adult learners: fear of regression (being put
back in the position of being a pupil again, having had
a "bad learning experience" at school).

Introvert embarrassed by role-playing and speaking to
the whole group?

Under pressure to learn English? (This might stem from
the need to pass an examination or be an essential
professional requirement.)

Other problems such as pressure of time, difficulties at
work, domestic problems, and so on.

END OF TERM ENCOUNTER

A-2

Focus: Awareness of yourself as a teacher in relation to your students, your colleagues, and your subject

Materials: Copies of page 86

Comment

The "End of Term Encounter" is intended for practicing teachers. It is not a classroom activity, so headings such as "In Class" are not relevant. The encounter is most suitable for the end of a term or school year when it is natural for teachers to reflect on what they have been doing in class and where they stand in relation to their profession. Nevertheless, there is no reason why the activity should not be done at any other time during the term or in the vacation.

The encounter is ideal as an activity in Teacher Development programs. All you need are copies of the list of points on page 86. On the other hand, you can also do the encounter alone by simply reading and reflecting on the points it contains, or you can discuss the points with a colleague you feel close to or with a good friend.

Some teachers may want to read the whole list, perhaps making notes as they go, before discussing anything. Others may prefer to read and then discuss the items point by point. There is no right or wrong way here. Do the encounter in the way that feels best to you. Omit any points you feel really uncomfortable with. Remember that the purpose of the encounter is to help you improve your teaching through awareness and reflection, not to make you feel bad about yourself.

Christopher Sion

§

The End of Term Encounter

Think of and discuss some or all of the following points:

1. A student you would (or will) be very sorry to lose from one of your classes and another student you cannot wait to be rid of

2. A technical point in your teaching you would like to improve and one you feel satisfied with, perhaps even proud of

3. Something you do in class that you want to stop doing and something else you want to start doing

4. A new technique you want to try: Which class will it be suitable for? When will be a good time?

5. A book or article about teaching you want to read: Why haven't you read it yet? When will you be able to open it?

6. Something in class you ignore: Are you justified in ignoring it? If not, what are you going to do about it?

7. A colleague you would like to see the back of and a colleague you would offer a job to if you ran your own school: Why do you feel this way about these colleagues? What do your feelings tell you about yourself?

8. What would you change at the school you teach in if you were the Director of Studies? Have you considered discussing these points with your Director of Studies? When would a good moment be to raise the issue?

9. Would you like to be a student in your own classes? Why (not)?

10. Have you ever told a lie or a white lie in class? Was it justified? What would you say if the same situation occurred again?

11. Something about the subject you teach that you would like to have clarified and something about which you feel your knowledge is thorough

12. A lesson or activity you have done once too often and should stop or revise: When are you going to improve or replace it? Have you any ideas for what exactly you are going to do?

13. When was the last time you attended a teacher training workshop, seminar, or lecture? Are you getting enough input to keep your teaching vital?

14. Some bad feedback you had: Was it justified?

15. Some good feedback you had that makes you feel really good to recall

16. What important points for improving your teaching has this encounter not touched on? What remains unsaid?

17. All in all, what is the next step for you in becoming a better teacher?

Focus: Revitalization of your teaching

Materials: Copies of the "Teacher's Roadworthy Test" and of the interpretation of it on pages 88–89.

Comment

This amusing little activity is intended for practicing teachers. It is described here for use in in-service teacher training courses and teacher development programs.

Before Class

Make copies of pages 88–89.

In Class

1. Brainstorm points that a garage should check when a car is serviced or goes for a roadworthy test.

2. Ask the teachers how many "teaching miles" they have done since their last "teaching service." Expect answers like "Thousands!" or "Far too many!"

3. Divide the group into pairs or small groups. Distribute copies of the Teacher's Roadworthy Test and ask the teachers to read through it and to discuss what the various points suggest to them.

4. Ask each teacher to give one example of what he or she understands by the points. For example, John picks "How good are your headlights?" and explains that for him it suggests "Have you got clear objectives? Do you know where you are going?" Johanna selects "Is your radio tuned properly?" For her this implies checking that the audio-visual equipment she uses in class is in good working order.

5. Distribute copies of our interpretation of the Teacher's Roadworthy Test from page 89.

6. Finish the activity by asking the teachers to reflect on one aspect of their teaching that they intend to improve.

Mike Lavery and Christopher Sion

§

Teacher's Roadworthy Test

Read through this list of questions. Think of yourself as a vehicle for language transmission. What do the points suggest to you? When you have finished reading, discuss your interpretation with a partner.

1. Have you checked your ignition?

2. Are your seat-belts in good working order?

3. Have you checked your reclining seats?

4. When did you last check your brakes?

5. Is your radio tuned properly?

6. Is your exhaust in good condition?

7. When did you last fill up with gasoline?

8. Do you change gears at the right time?

9. Is your clutch slipping?

10. Have you got a well-stocked first-aid kit?

11. Do you always carry a spare tire in case you have a puncture?

12. How good are your headlights?

13. Are your mirrors properly adjusted?

14. When were you last washed?

15. Does your hair need an oil change?

16. Have you inspected your chassis for rust?

17. When did you last change your spark plugs?

18. Ready to go? Or does your battery need recharging?

What the Teacher's Roadworthy Test suggests to us, the authors:

1. Have you checked your ignition?
   (Do your lessons start first time?)

2. Are your seat-belts in good working order?
   (Is your class safe for students to express themselves freely and honestly?)

3. Have you checked your reclining seats?
   (Is the atmosphere in your classes relaxed?)

4. When did you last check your brakes?
   (Can you stop yourself talking?)

5. Is your radio tuned properly?
   (Do you really listen to your students or are their voices lost in the engine noise?)

6. Is your exhaust in good condition?
   (Do you allow students to let off steam in class?)

7. When did you last fill up on gasoline?
   (What was the last professional input you received? When is the next input likely to be?)

8. Do you change gears at the right time?
   (Are you responsive to your students' needs? Or are you automatic?)

9. Is your clutch slipping?
   (Do your classes sometimes get out of control?)

10. Have you got a well-stocked first-aid kit?
    (Are you thrown off balance by the unexpected or can you cope with emergencies?)

11. Do you always carry a spare tire in case you have a puncture?
    (Are you adequately prepared with alternative material?)

12. How good are your headlights?
    (Can you see the problems that exist in your classes? Are you blinding the students with your own high beam?)

13. Are your mirrors properly adjusted?
    (Can you see what's going on behind your back? Have you got any teaching "blind spots"?)

14. When were you last washed?
    (Does your appearance affect your students' perception of your performance?)

15. Does your hair need an oil change?
    (Is it time to change your hairstyle, invest in some new clothes, and generally change your image?)

16. Have you inspected your chassis for rust?
    (Are *you* getting rusty? Do you need a refresher course?)

17. When did you last change your spark plugs?
    (Is that "little spark" there when you teach? If not, what can you do to rekindle it?)

18. Ready to go? Or does your battery need recharging?
    (When are you going to recharge *yourself*? What are you waiting for?)

Focus: Developing an awareness of the fact that students often know far more than they are credited with and that even when students do not know an answer, they can easily be led to find it; changing the image of the student as a "vessel to be filled"

Materials: None

Comment

The idea of elicitation as it is understood here is to draw vocabulary from the students themselves as far as possible.

Points to bear in mind are:

a. Elicitation motivates the students by gently pressuring them to work actively.
b. If vocabulary is learned via association or as part of an activity it is more likely to be retained than if it is learned in a vacuum.
c. A further reason why elicitation is effective is because it provides students with the pleasure of seeking and finding.
d. If the students have difficulty in trying to find a word you should tell them what it is before they really get stuck. Despite the value of finding the answer for themselves, if you make them wait too long the students will stop looking.
e. Use the elicitation methods liberally, but beware of using them too much. If you introduce *all* new words and answer *all* vocabulary questions via one of the techniques, your students will soon start losing interest.

Before Class

In the case of Method 9, prepare the code.

In Class

Method 1. If you want to introduce a new word, such as *stamp,* to an elementary class, give them the word letter by letter. Build the word up on the board as follows:

The word has five letters.
The first letter is *S.*
The last letter is *P.*
The middle letter is *A.*
The other two letters are *M* and *T.*

```
_ _ _ _ _
S _ _ _ _
S _ _ _ P
S _ A _ P
S T A M P
```

Method 2. Proceed as in Method 1, but work successively from the first letter to the second, the third, and fourth and so on to the end of the word.

Method 3. A further adaptation of Method 1: this time work backwards from the last letter to the second last, continuing letter by letter until you reach the beginning.

Method 4. Scramble the letters a word is composed of. For example, teach or review the word *calendar* by writing *A C D L N E R A* on the board. Then ask the students to find the word by rearranging the letters. If the students have difficulties, help them by telling them that the word begins with *C.* Should students produce correct English words, which are, however, not the word you are looking for, congratulate them on finding alternatives, but tell them there is another word in those letters which is the one you want.

Method 5. Introduce the words by giving either the vowels or the consonants. It is worth noting that giving only the vowels tends to be far more difficult to do than supplying the consonants. For example:

_ E _ _ _ I _ U E = T E C H N I Q U E (with missing consonants)
C _ M P _ T _ R = C O M P U T E R (with missing vowels)

Method 6. Use a + sign to indicate the vowels and a − sign to indicate the consonants. For example, ELE-PHANT is presented as + − + − − + − −. Tell students to proceed by asking questions such as: "Is the second vowel an *I*?" "Is the first consonant a *K*?" "Is the last letter in the second half of the alphabet?"

Method 7. Use a mixture of questions, puns, riddles, and so on. Imagine you want to elicit the name *Scotland Yard*. You may do this by asking questions such as the following:

> "Ivanhoe" was written by Sir Walter . . . .?
> SCOTT → SCOT
> When aircraft return to earth they . . . .?
> LAND → SCOTLAND
> Thirty-six inches make one . . . .?
> YARD → SCOTLAND YARD

To elicit *Empire State* from a high intermediate class ask:

> What's the thirteenth letter of the alphabet?
> M → EM
> A dead body may be cremated on a funeral . . . .?
> PYRE → EMPIRE
> Another word meaning *condition*.
> STATE → EMPIRE STATE

The possibilities are endless. A word of warning, however: be sure to keep the rhythm moving or you will risk boring the class. If examples such as the two above take more than about 20 seconds, you are going too slowly.

Method 8. With monolingual classes you can use translation for different parts of compound words. For example, to elicit the word *playboy* from a class of German speakers ask:

> What's the English word for *spielen*? PLAY
> What's the English word for *Junge*? BOY

Method 9. Use simple codes to introduce and review vocabulary. The easiest is to use 1 for *A*, 2 for *B*, 3 for *C*, and so on, through the alphabet to *Z*, which is 26. Thus, 8 15 21 19 5 = H O U S E. This technique is particularly popular with classes of children, who relish the idea of something cryptic. If the students cannot crack the code for themselves, explain the principle on which the code is based and ask the students to decode whatever it is you want them to work on. The disadvantages, however, are that more complex codes require preparation before class and can take a long time for the students to decipher.

Method 10. Use mime and gestures. Point up to indicate *up* and down for *down*. Hold up two fingers to prompt the particle *to* and four fingers to indicate the preposition *for*. The humorous associations thus produced are a most effective aid to learning.

Christopher Sion

§

HE CORRECT BALANCE

Focus: Developing a variety of approaches to error correction; assisting students to monitor their own performance in the target language

Materials: See the methods described below

Comment

When should we correct? How much should we correct? What should we correct? How should we correct? Who should we correct? Why? What evidence is there that error correction is an effective means of improving communicative competence?

I know that when I am attempting my first faltering words in a new language the last thing I want is to be told that I am not getting it right; but it is no less true that I resent it when I am allowed to get away with my errors persistently. If nobody corrects me, I feel nobody cares. When I discover that I have been getting it wrong for years while nobody has bothered to react, I feel I have been let down.

If my teachers want to help me, they can do so by gently drawing my attention to my mistakes and then guiding me to the correct forms. I want encouragement, not flattery, and certainly not abuse.

My experience as a teacher, however, often leaves me feeling that the very errors I most assiduously try to iron out are those errors that the students seem most determined to go on making. I do not know what negative subliminal learning cues I am projecting unconsciously. I do know that when I ask them, my students invariably reply that they definitely do want to be corrected.

Finding the means and the moment to correct effectively depends on keen observation, patience, and sensitivity to language and learners. No two students learn in exactly the same way. Effective correction requires intuition, tact, and good timing. It is a question of finding the correct balance.

Before Class

Any preparation required is minimal and is implicitly referred to in the methods described below.

In Class

Method 1. Tape record part or all of a lesson. Do not interrupt the students as they talk. Analyze the recording after class. Decide which language points to focus on at the next lesson on the basis of the mistakes that were made.

Method 2. Do not interrupt the students while they are talking, but note the errors they make. Discuss these errors with the class after the activity is over.

Method 3. After introducing or reviewing a particular teaching point, tell the students to monitor each other. Every time the students notice class members making the mistake in question, they should quietly draw attention to it.

Method 4. Use large cards to draw attention to errors. These need to be prepared before class in anticipation of likely errors at the level you are teaching. For example, with low intermediate classes, use a large *S* to indicate "There is an *S* missing." Or use a big question mark to indicate "That's not the way to form questions."

Method 5. Use your fingers as prompts. For example, a student says "You eat at home?" meaning "Do you eat at home?" Hold up one hand, pointing at four fingers to represent the four words "You eat at home." Using gestures, show the class that one finger is intended to represent one word and that there is a missing word (represented in this case by the thumb) in the sentence "You eat at home?" Do not tell the students what the missing word is, but silently draw the word from them using gestures. (Like so many things that are very easy to do in practice, this is extremely difficult to describe in words.)

Method 6. Whisper the correct form to students from behind as they speak. It might take you a while to get the feel of the mechanics of this method but it is well worth the effort. Whisper correction is far more elegant and far less of an interruption than the "head-on" approach. (Obviously you cannot expect to correct all the students all the time using this method. This does not make it less effective.)

Method 7. This method may be described as Variable Correction: have some sessions in which you correct the students very strictly and others in which there is hardly any correction at all. Consult the students about the extent they want to be corrected. Some want to be pushed the whole time; others want less pressure at the end of the day.

Method 8. When a mistake has been made, raise your eyebrows, look aghast or amazed, and simply let the students work out what is wrong for themselves. The students will frequently find the correct version if you give them a little time.

Method 9. Hold campaigns against particular errors; for instance, if you are working on getting an English *h* sound, have a big *H* permanently on the board and hit it when the error arises.

Method 10. Have the students make a list of all the points they want to stop getting wrong. Use this list as the basis of a personal checklist that the students can use to monitor their own work; for example: "I have not said *much* when I mean *many*" or "I have not written 'If I would have' when I mean 'If I had.'"

Method 11. Pass "Hot Cards," little pieces of paper with messages, to individual students. Hot cards can be used as follows:

a. Write the students' mistakes exactly as they are made, one per hot card, and distribute them so that the students can correct them. The cards may be distributed as the activity progresses or saved until it is finished. Examples of hot card messages might be: Will you a cup of coffee? This sandwich tastes well!

b. Instead of writing only the mistakes, write the correct version of what the students were trying to say. For example: Do you want a cup of coffee? This sandwich tastes good!

c. In addition to points *a* and *b,* use hot cards to *praise* students for correct structures, correctly pronounced words, and so on. (It is interesting to note how much attention is paid to the question of correction and how little to praise in educational theory and practice.)

Method 12. Write on the board a selection of errors that have been made. Then brainstorm improvements with the class. Let the students correct the errors wherever possible. Only tell them the correct version as a last resort.

Method 13. Repeat the student's statement with a bemused, incredulous echo, for example: "Your daughter is nine*ty* years old?!" or ask for clarification: "Do you really mean you had soap for lunch?" As in the case of Method 8, given a little time you will be amazed at the extent to which students are able to correct themselves.

Method 14. Ignore the mistake. The students will learn (or not) in their own good time without any correction at all!

Author's Note

Most of the methods described above were collected by Pilgrims teachers at a teaching workshop in Canterbury, England, in the late 1970s. I should like to thank: Denny Packard for adding a major contribution to the original list; Gerry Kenny for drawing my attention to "Whisper Correction," which comes from Charles Curran's "Community Language Learning." *Method 5*, "Finger Correction," comes from Caleb Gattegno's *Silent Way*.

Christopher Sion

§

FEEDBACK: THEORY AND PRACTICE

Appendix A: / TEACHER DEVELOPMENT / Time: 15–30 minutes per method

Focus: For teachers to develop an on-going awareness of their teaching; assistance in discovering that a teacher's opinion of what is taking place in his or her lessons does not always correspond with what the students think.

Materials: Copies of the figures and questionnaire on pages 97–98; if duplicating facilities are in short supply in your teaching situation, tell the students to make their own simple sketches of the figures

Comment

I wonder how many teachers there are who never ask for feedback from their students at all. Hands up those teachers who only request feedback at the *end* of a course when it is too late to take it into account. In my experience, many teachers only hold feedback sessions when they feel there is something unsatisfactory with their teaching, while others tend to ask for students' opinions exclusively when things are going well and comments are bound to be flattering.

I would like to suggest that gathering feedback should be an integral part of all educational courses. I believe there should be a continuing dialogue between teachers and students. The purpose of this dialogue is twofold. Firstly, to help teachers improve the way they are coming across; secondly, to help students clarify their thoughts and feelings about what they are being asked to do in the classroom.

It is important to note that the term "feedback" in this context means more than simply "gathering information about what the students think and feel." "Feedback" implies *modifying or correcting your teaching approach in the light of what your students reveal to you about their impressions of it.* There is no point whatsoever in aimlessly inquiring what the students think of your lessons unless you go on to take their comments into account in your teaching. Naturally this does not imply that you have to agree with everything they say; only that you should take it into consideration.

Finally, no matter what negative and hostile reactions you might encounter, *there is no need to let negative feedback upset you.* Negative feedback does not mean you are a failure; it simply provides you with an opportunity to improve your classroom performance. If a student complains, "The level's too low for me," step up the level for him or her. You have learned that that student wants a challenge. If a student writes, "There's too

much grammar," ask yourself if this is a fair comment and if it is possible to do more communicative activities. Most important, be sure to check whether an opinion expressed by one student is shared by the majority of the class. You may wish to redraw and enlarge the art so that each drawing fills an 8½ by 11 inch sheet of paper.

Before Class

Make copies of the materials you require for whichever method you choose to use.

In Class

The following five methods of gathering feedback may all be approached either as activities to be discussed in class, or as written work to be collected by the teacher. If you have a low-level class in which the students are unable to express themselves adequately in written English, tell them they can write in their own language, assuming, or course, that you can read it or can find someone else to translate it for you. Written feedback should only be corrected if a student specifically requests it.

Method 1: The Feedback Bottle. Distribute copies of "The Feedback Bottle." Tell the students to imagine that they are on a desert island, desperately wanting to communicate what they are feeling and badly needing contact. The only way to establish contact with anybody is to write a message, put it in a bottle, and throw it out to sea. Tell the students to write their "messages" (*i.e.,* their feedback) in their bottles and then throw them to you at the front of the class. (You could learn a lot about how the students feel from the way they throw.)

Method 2: The Feedback Heart. Tell the students to fill in everything they liked about the course inside the heart and any positive suggestions for improvement outside it.

Method 3: The Feedback Head. Ask the students to write all their impressions of the course inside the head.

Method 4: Thinking and Feeling. Copy the heart on one side of a sheet of paper and the head on the other. Ask the students to write what they *feel* about the course in the heart and what they *think* about the course in the head. (This method is generally only suitable with high level classes.)

Method 5: Questionnaire. Distribute the questionnaire and ask the students to fill it in. The questions are structured in such a way as to provide an exceptionally valuable source of information concerning the students' impressions of themselves and of the class.

Author's Notes

Some teachers believe you should not ask the students to put their names on their feedback, or that they should at least be given the choice of signing their comments or not. Personally I prefer to ask for the students' signatures. I explain that this is more honest than pretending that the students have the protection of anonymity, when in fact it is frequently impossible to avoid identifying the students by their handwriting.

The notion that failure should be redefined or reframed as feedback comes from Neuro-Linguistic Programming (NLP).

Christopher Sion

§

Feedback Bottle

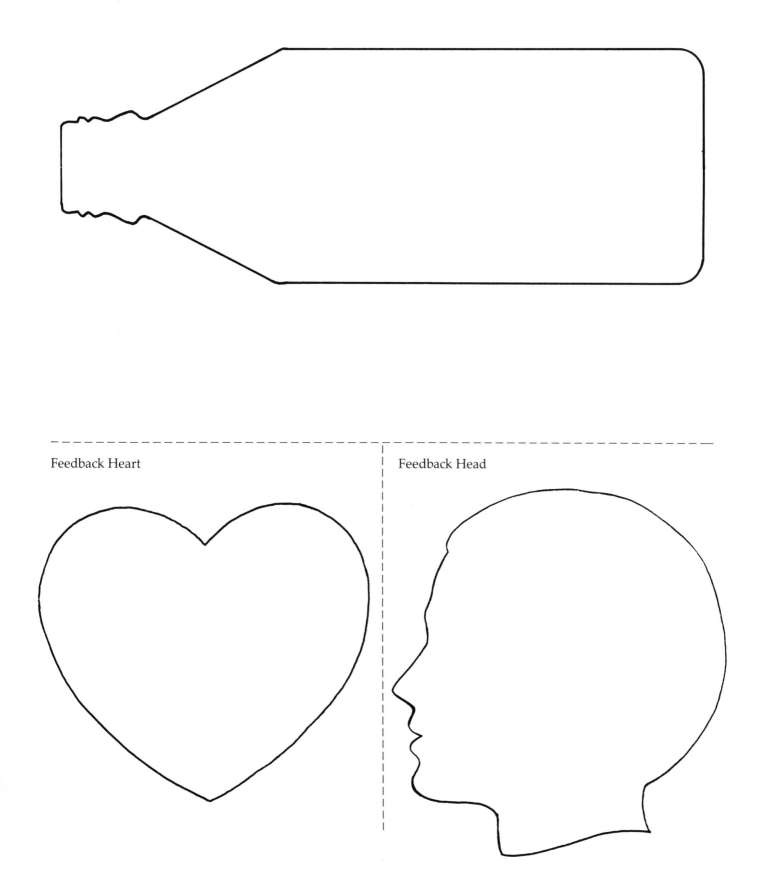

Feedback Heart

Feedback Head

Questionnaire

1. The best way to motivate me is . . . . .

2. The class as a whole is . . . . .

3. The material is . . . . .

4. When I am corrected I feel . . . . .

5. When I am not corrected I feel . . . . .

6. English is . . . . .

7. When I tell other people about this class I say . . . . .

8. A good question for a feedback questionnaire like this would be . . . . .

   My answer to this question would be . . . . .

THE WRITING'S ON THE WALL

Appendix A: / TEACHER DEVELOPMENT / Time: 15–30 minutes

Focus: Feedback

Materials: Large sheets of paper, two sheets per student

Comment

The aim of this activity is to assist teachers in becoming more aware of students' learning needs.

In Class

1. Tell the students you have an unusual discussion topic: Does anybody recall ever writing on walls when they were young children? What did they write? Where? Why? Were they found out and punished? Prompt, help, and coax the students as necessary by asking, for example, if they know any mischievous children, and if any of these children have ever been known to write on walls. (As students may occasionally be cautious about sharing their recollections immediately, it is well worth devoting time to this warm-up phase. Proceed gently and put the students at their ease so that they feel comfortable about "opening up.")

2. Ask the students if they ever have the urge to write on walls today. What would they like to say? If the students were free to write whatever they wanted, on whichever walls they wanted, without fear of being reprimanded, what would they choose to express? (If anyone is honest enough to confess to being a graffiti artist, thank that person for being open about it. This is not the place for reproach.)

3. Have the class work in small groups. Tell the students you are going to give them the opportunity to express their feelings freely on a wall! Distribute one

sheet of chart paper to each student. Tell the students to imagine that the sheet of paper is a "wall" and they are to write or draw whatever they wish on these handouts and then discuss what they have written in their groups. Keep a close watch on the discussions, providing help as necessary.

4. Give each student a clean sheet of chart paper. Explain to the class that you would now like to use the activity to gather feedback about the course. Ask the students to write their impressions of the course as graffiti on their "Feedback Walls."

5. *Method 1:* Finish off the activity by asking the students to tell you what they think of the course. What do they find particularly valuable? What would they like to have changed? The students should use their "Feedback Walls" as the basis of this discussion, adding further details as they wish. Ask the students to explain what they mean and give further details where they can only if they wish to. Listen closely to what the students tell you without becoming defensive if you hear something you do not want to hear.

Method 2: Collect the "Walls" (from step 4) and take them home with you for careful consideration and reflection. (Bear in mind that many students are likely to be more frank in expressing their opinions privately on paper than in an open discussion. For this reason the best policy is probably to do both Methods 1 *and* 2.)

Author's Notes

a. If you want to use this activity only as an exercise in expressing and discussing opinions, not as a feedback exercise, do only steps 1, 2, and 3. In this case, you may wish to conclude the activity by displaying the "Walls" around the classroom. Allow the students time to move around the room reading and discussing each other's opinions.
b. The idea of writing on walls may also be found in a forthcoming book of mine provisionally entitled *Lead-Ins and Fade-Outs*.

Mike Lavery

Editor's Note

You may have to modify what is set out in step 1 a little if you attempt this activity with classes of children.

§

Focus: Classroom observation; appraising teaching performance

Materials: Copies of the checklist on pages 103–104

Comment

This checklist may be used in several different ways:

a. To monitor your own teaching performance. After a lesson, analyze what you did in class with reference to the checklist. (If you are able to use a video or audio recording of yourself actually teaching your lesson for this purpose, so much the better!)

b. Ask a colleague to come and observe your teaching and use the checklist to give you feedback.

c. As an aid in observing teachers or teacher trainees in practice. Knowing what to look for will guide your perception of all the different features of a lesson. The presentation of the "Classroom Observation Checklist" as described below is written from this point of view. It is invaluable as an instrument of analysis in observing teacher trainees, both pre-service and in-service, in teaching practice (see step 4).

Before Class

Make copies of the checklist.

In Class

1. Brainstorm the subject "Points to look for when observing classes." Write the students' ideas on the board, adding important details, prompting and commenting as you write. The points to focus on are included in the checklist on the following pages.

2. Distribute copies of the checklist on pages 103–104. Have the students work in small groups. Tell the students to discuss which items on the checklist (or on the board) they feel are the key points in teaching and any points on the checklist that have not been dealt with during the brainstorming session.

3. Ask each student to say which point he or she regards as the most important aspect of the teaching/learning process and why. Accept all responses but encourage the students to explain *why* they feel as they do.

4. Arrange for the students to observe a teacher in class and/or give a practice lesson to be analyzed using the checklist. As mentioned above, the students addressed in this activity are teacher trainees. Actually being able to use the "Classroom Observation Checklist" for teacher training will depend on the training situation in which you find yourself and the opportunities available for teaching practice and classroom observation.

Author's Notes

a. This checklist is based on two handouts I found at Pilgrims Language Courses summer school in Canterbury, England in 1978. I do not know who prepared them so I cannot give a proper acknowledgement. I have added several points of my own, and have consulted the artjcles by L. Baltra and R. Freudenstein in *Teacher Training* (Ed. Susan Holden, Modern English Publications, 1979).

b. I hope the checklist will prove useful to: teachers, teacher trainers, and examiners who have to observe and assess others' classes; teachers and teacher trainees who wish to reflect on and improve their own classroom performance.

c. Please note that there is a certain amount of overlap between some of the points on the checklist. The points are *not* presented in any suggested order of importance.

Christopher Sion

§

Points to Look for When Observing Classes

1. Some basic points:

   a. Can everybody see?

   b. How is the seating arranged? (Rows? Horseshoe formation?)

   c. Is the teacher's voice clear?

   d. Is the teacher's writing legible?

2. Effective use of board, books, and all other aids and materials.

3. Proportion of "Teacher Talking Time" to "Student Talking Time."

4. To what extent is the class conducted in English? Is there any translation, and if so, is it justified?

5. What is the point of what is being taught? Is it clear? Valuable? Relevant?

6. The lesson plan:

   a. How much preparation is required to give a lesson like this?

   b. How systematic is the lesson?

   c. How flexible is the teacher when the class does not proceed as planned?

   d. Is there any variation in the way different exercises and activities are presented?

   e. Tempo? Momentum?

7. What use is made of work already covered? Are grammar and vocabulary reviewed or does the teacher take it for granted that whatever had been covered previously has been remembered?

8. Is comprehension checked thoroughly?

9. Correction:

   a. Are students given the chance to correct their own mistakes?

   b. Is there any student to student correction?

   c. What is the teacher's attitude to students who haven't understood despite repeated explanation?

   d. Do the teacher's corrections carry an element of reproach or anger? (In other words, when the teacher corrects a student, does the teacher try to make the student feel bad and stupid for not having known the correct answer?)

   e. Are students praised when they get it right?

   f. Is the praise mechanical or genuinely enthusiastic?

10. General Classroom atmosphere:

    a. Is the lesson lively and personal?

    b. Is the atmosphere authoritarian or democratic? (Is the teacher generally democratic but nevertheless "selectively authoritarian," so that one or two students are unfairly treated?)

    c. How much laughter do you hear in class?

    d. Is the situation under control or out of control?

11. Are there discipline problems? If so, how are these coped with? If not, how does the teacher maintain order?

12. Body language. Details to look for here include:

    a. General appearance.

    b. Does the teacher have any distracting mannerisms?

    c. How does the teacher stand, sit, move, and gesture?

    d. Eye contact. (Does the teacher look at the students when talking to them?)

    e. Is the quality of the teacher's voice pleasant and steady or harsh and nervous?

    f. All in all, does the teacher project a positive or a negative image?

13. How motivated are the students? What does the teacher do to keep them motivated? And how motivated is the teacher?

14. Is the teacher the master of what is being taught? Does the teacher make a confident impression and seem to understand the subject? Does he or she make mistakes? If so, how does he or she react?

15. Are the objectives underlying the lesson clear? Are the objectives achieved? Why (not)? Is anything achieved, perhaps by accident, that is not specified in the objectives?

16. Content:

    a. Which structures and functions are focused on?

    b. Are grammatical points explained briefly and clearly or is there a preoccupation with grammatical theory at the expense of communicative practice?

17. Individualization:

    a. Is the teacher adaptable to the personal needs of the students?

    b. Does the teacher appear to know the students well and appreciate individual differences in their personalities and learning styles?

    c. Are the students often called by their names?

18. Involvement:

    a. Are *all* the students involved?

    b. Do they *all* participate?

    c. Is the atmosphere safe for students to contribute without having to worry about making a mistake or being laughed at?

19. Teacher's attitude to students who don't participate or participate not quite as expected:

    a. Patient?

    b. Encouraging?

    c. Accepting or rejecting?

    d. Invading?

    e. Or are these students simply ignored?

20. Is the teacher imposing his or her will on the class? If so, is this justified?

21. All in all:

    a. Do the students seem to be enjoying the lesson?

    b. What exactly are the students learning?

    c. Would *you* like to be a student in this class? Why (not)?

22. If you were teaching this class, what precisely would you do differently? Why?

APPENDIX B

MINI-RECIPES

"Brevity is the soul of wit."
William Shakespeare

WORD OF EXPLANATION

The mini-recipes are new or unusual teaching ideas which are economically expressed in a handful of words. Each one offers no more than the germ of an idea. The responsibility for developing the details is passed on to the teacher. The mini-recipes are intended to encourage teachers to think for themselves and make use of their own creativity and common sense in planning their lessons. I am convinced that by investing a little time, reflection, and effort in careful preparation, almost all teachers will be able to meet the challenge and will positively enjoy bringing the mini-recipes to life.

The mini-recipes stand in sharp contrast to the full-length recipes which are carefully set out step by step. The mini-recipes, each of which is described in a maximum of only seventeen words, are like seeds which have yet to be planted. It is up to you to cultivate them and watch them develop.

Mini-recipes arise spontaneously from seminars, workshops, reading, reflecting, and casual conversations with colleagues. Their origins are essentially magical and mysterious. A primary source of inspiration is everyday life. Look around you. What can you see? What can you hear? What have you just been doing? In my case, I've just been reading today's mail. My mind starts playing with the idea of a "Morning Mail" recipe.

Stop reading for a minute or two and ask yourself how *you* would turn "Morning Mail" into a recipe? Once you can think of something, anything at all, no matter how simple or seemingly unoriginal it might appear, make a few notes about it. Try to answer the following questions: What level and language functions is it suitable for? How much time do you estimate it will require in class? Do you need any materials? What must you do before class? How will you warm up the class before the activity starts? Is there any new vocabulary that needs to be taught? What tenses or other structures will the students need to do the exercise? Do any grammar points need reviewing? Will the class be split into pairs or small groups? Are there any organizational problems to consider in setting up the activity?

Whether you have a lot of teaching experience or only a little, if you feel hesitant about the mini-recipes try dividing them into three sets, "Yes," "No," and "Maybe." Begin by trying one or two of the more appealing ones, that you marked "Yes," until you feel confident enough to try the "Maybes."

The mini-recipes appended here are intended to fire your imagination and inspire the creative teacher in you. If they attract you, try them. If they confuse you, dismiss them. Even if you reject half of the minis, you will still be left with over thirty new ideas that you can use, and that means over thirty new activities for enriching your classwork.

There is no need to be a boring teacher! Have fun and good luck!

DESIRING AND IMAGINING

1. If you could be rich (but not famous) or famous (but not rich), which would you choose?

   Claudia Kniep

2. Have the students design their own classroom.

   Peter Thompson

3. Describe in detail what students will look like and how they will dress in ten years' time.

   Peter Grundy

4. Write down all your unfulfilled wishes. Mark those which seem impossible to fulfill. Are they *really* impossible?

   Mike Lavery

5. If you ruled the world for one day . . .

   Claudia Kniep

6. Distribute maps of continents with only rivers and mountains marked. Students divide area into ten new countries.

   Peter Grundy

7. Ask the class to imagine they have adopted a child and decide on a name for it.

   Mike Lavery

8. There are certain things (feelings, insights, emotions) for which there is no language in words . . .

   Gerry Kenny

9. Imagine no money existed. Devise a system of barter; for example, one spear equals five chickens.

   Mike Lavery

§

PERSONAL EXPERIENCE

1. Which historical dates do you remember? Why?

    Katya Benjamin

2. Trace the history of your hairstyles. When did you change them and why.

    Lou Spaventa

3. Describe a favorite piece of clothing. How did you get it? Why do you like it?

    Heidi Yorkshire

4. List and discuss the most important people at various periods in your life.

    Kathleen Schlusmans

5. Students use slides/snapshots/postcards to give talks on their towns/countries/regions.

    Allan Ryding

6. Ask the students to describe their favorite teacher.

    Denny Packard

7. Students describe an eccentric uncle or aunt and then vote on whose example was the most eccentric.

    Bertrand Russell

8. Students describe in detail the strangest thing they have ever seen.

    Paul Docherty

9. Students mime objects from their past, like childhood possessions. Others ask questions to establish the objects' histories.

    Marjorie Baudains

10. List the most important years in your life and then discuss the most important event from each year.

    Kathleen Schlusmans

11. Which movie, video, or TV program would you want on a desert island? Why?

    Liz Dixey

12. Find ten adjectives to describe a favorite piece of clothing. Does it reflect your personality?

    Katya Benjamin

13. Each student prepares twenty questions which another uses to interview him/her. Answers must contain new information.

    Carlos Maeztu

14. Think of ten questions that you would personally not want to answer.

    John Thompson

§

CREATIVE WRITING

1. Write the name, nationality, and occupation that are most unlike your own. Explain your choices.

   Peter Grundy

2. Write comprehension questions referring to picture stories on cards. Students match questions and stories and find answers.

   Pat Charalambides

3. Write sentences from the letters of your home town: <u>V</u>ictor <u>A</u>nd <u>L</u>ola <u>E</u>at <u>N</u>ational <u>C</u>ooking <u>I</u>n <u>A</u>merica

   Bryan Robinson

4. How many English words can you make from the letters of your name?

   Jean-Paul Creton

5. Write your own epitaph or obituary.

   Martin Worth

6. A day after a role-play, present class with a "newspaper report" of that role-play.

   Patrick Gibben

7. Students suggest their own examination paper. Which questions would they want to answer? And which not? Why?

   Kathleen Schlusmans

8. For "student-centered feedback" have your class write their own progress reports.

   Christopher Sion

9. Elementary students write as many English words as they can in five minutes. They compare in pairs.

   Mike Lavery

10. Write descriptions of pictures from picture stories on cards. Students to match pictures.

    Pat Charalambides

11. Students to make six to ten changes in a text without altering the main sense.

    Mike Lavery

12. Have the students write an entry, real or imaginary, for themselves in "Who's Who."

    Kathleen Schlusmans

13. Distribute large sheets of paper. The students write/draw whatever they want on them and then discuss.

    Katya Benjamin

§

FACTS AND EXPLANATIONS

1. Explain why there are 24 hours in a day. Devise an alternative time scale.

   Bryan Robinson

2. "Winter is caused by cold weather." What *is* winter caused by?

   Christopher Sion

3. Why is London, New York, Peking (or any other city) where it is?

   Alison Baxter

4. What makes classical music classical?

   Kathleen Schlusmans

5. What is creativity and what would the world be without it?

   Denny Packard

6. Explain the rules of a game or sport. Which rules would you like to change? Why?

   Martin Worth

7. How do you iron a shirt?

   Peter Grundy

8. Recommend ways governments could economize and become more efficiently run.

   Denny Packard

§

ENGLISH FOR SPECIAL PURPOSES

1. Ask a class of secretaries, technicians, clerks, etc. to describe their ideal day.

   Martin Worth

2. Have a class of technical students brainstorm *technical* applications of everyday objects (*e.g.*, a toothpick).

   Martin Worth

3. Have a class of business people talk in pairs about the applications of computers in their jobs.

   Christopher Sion

4. Tell a class of business students that a company has gone bankrupt and simply let them expand.

   Cynthia Beresford

5. Similarly . . . Why did the:
   product fail/succeed?
   workers strike?
   salesperson resign?
   Managing Director lose his/her job?

   Martin Worth

6. Have students make drawings of the settings they work in and use these as basis for mini-presentations.

   Christopher Sion

7. Ask a group of secretaries (or secretarial students) to describe their ideal boss.

   Martin Worth

8. Have a group of business people describe the best (and worst) secretaries they have ever encountered.

   Christopher Sion

§

TALKING AND CONVERSING

1. Think of ten ways in which you can improve your English.

    John Thompson

2. Draw a picture slowly. Have the class speculate what it is as you draw.

    Mario Rinvolucri

3. Students make a list of points on how (not to) raise children. Discuss.

    Denny Packard

4. Role-play: travel agents inform and advise tourists about resorts (travel, accommodation, amenities, climate, food, cost, etc.).

    Allan Ryding

5. Students tell partners the story of a comic strip (without showing it to them).

    Ray Janssens

6. Ask your students to discuss how creativity can best be fostered by the educational system.

    Denny Packard

7. Each student to tell a joke, which a classmate reports back to the group in indirect speech.

    René Bosewitz

8. Distribute sets of "language scraps" (for example, tickets, receipts, forms, etc.) as the basis for character sketches.

    Allan Ryding

9. Ask the class to discuss why students smoke.

    Denny Packard

§

FOR TEACHERS AND TEACHER TRAINEES

1. Expand a mini-recipe into a full teaching recipe or lesson plan (and vice versa).

   Kathleen Schlusmans

2. Find somewhere quiet. Visualize yourself giving a lesson that makes you feel good before you start teaching.

   Katya Benjamin

3. Teacher trainees recall activities done during a lesson. Which did they warm to? Which left them cold?

   Mike Lavery

4. Have teacher trainees explain and analyze: "The English teacher came to class but no students showed up."

   Denny Packard

5. Play background music to create a relaxed atmosphere as students enter the classroom and during group work.

   Mike Lavery

6. Open the dictionary anywhere. Run your finger down the page. Stop. Read the headword. Prepare from this.

   Gerry Kenny

7. Put copies of a text on students' seats before class. Curiosity will often make them read.

   Mike Lavery

8. Divide board into positive and negative areas. Students write feedback about course on appropriate area of board.

   Christopher Sion

§

PROVOCATIVE AND CONTROVERSIAL

1. Students list the typical contents of a dustbin in their countries.

   Peter Grundy

2. Ask class why students are like sheep and don't criticize anything, such as what you're saying now.

   René Bosewitz

3. Tell the class to prepare a set of ten "Devil's Commandments" based on immoral imperatives.

   Richard Baudains

4. Students devise a dowry system for an imaginary country. Is your daughter worth five tractors? A calculator?

   Mike Lavery

5. Ethnic races are like the colors of the rainbow. Where does blue stop and green begin?

   Franky Bulmer

6. Why are the middle classes so fat?

   Peter Grundy

§

INDEX

LANGUAGE FUNCTIONS

adjectives, practicing, 43
advice, giving, 14
agreeing and disagreeing, 52, 62, 78
asking and answering questions, 5, 6,
    20, 40, 42, 43, 56, 58, 68, 69
associations
    making, 54
    of words and music, 37
calculating, 71
categorizing vocabulary, 44, 69
checking information, 75
combining words into sentences, 66
comparing, 45
    ideas, 67
    personal information, 34
comparisons, making, 12
compiling information, 75
comprehension, listening, 36
conditional statements, expressing, 79
context, importance of in translations, 4
conversation, making, 18
creative writing, 19, 34
criticism, voicing, 59
decisions, making and evaluating, 75
denying, and persuading, 16
describing, 5, 7, 19, 45
    and imagining, 24, 42, 67
    and inventing, 23
developing awareness of register
    and importance of context in
    translations, 41
dialogues, writing, 64
disagreeing, and agreeing, 52, 62, 78
discussing, 9
evaluating
    judgments, 2
    and making decisions, 75
exchanging
    and comparing personal
        information, 34
    ideas, 24
    information, 72
explaining, 20
expressing
    agreement and disagreement, 52
    conditional statements, 79
    feelings, 28
    likes and dislikes, 5
    moral preferences, 12
    opinions, 10, 58, 62
    preferences, 59
    spatial relations, 25
feelings, expressing, 28
giving
    advice, 14
    instructions, 25
grammar, reviewing, 13
ideas
    comparing, 67
    exchanging, 24

identifying and practicing sounds, 32,
    38
imagining, 7
    and describing, 24, 42, 67
indirect speech, 79
information
    compiling, checking, and sharing, 75
    exchanging and comparing, 34, 72
    passing, 31
    presenting, 47, 62
instructions, giving, 25
intensive listening, 70
inventing, 19
    and describing, 23
judgments
    evaluating, 2
    making, 2
justifying, 21
likes and dislikes, expressing, 5
listening, 70
    comprehension, 36
making and evaluating decisions, 75
making and responding to requests, 20
making associations, 54
    of words and music, 37
making comparisons, 12
making conversation, 18
making judgments, 2
making suggestions, 59
moral preferences, expressing, 12
narrating, 26, 29, 55, 60, 79
newspaper headlines, writing, 78
note taking, 31
opinions, expressing, 10, 58, 62
passing information, 31
persuading, 42, 75
    and denying, 16
practicing
    adjectives, 43
    numbers, 71
    vocabulary, 48, 49
    writing, 22
    sounds, 32, 38
preferences, expressing, 59
presenting information, 47, 62
questions, asking and answering, 5, 6,
    20, 40, 42, 43, 56, 58, 68, 69
reading for gist, 36
recollecting, 5
register, developing awareness of, 4
requesting information, 25
requests, making and responding to, 20
responding to requests, 20
reviewing
    grammar, 13
    two- and three-word verbs, 47
    vocabulary, 22, 70
sentences
    combining words into, 66
    writing, 60
socializing, 8, 72
sounds, identifying and practicing, 32,
    38

spatial relations, expressing, 25
speculating, 9, 10, 13, 21, 23, 28, 45,
    64, 66, 69, 79
speech, indirect, 79
suggesting, 59, 62
summarizing, 31
talking about the past, 28
translations, importance of register and
    context in, 4
verbs, two- and three-word, 47
vocabulary
    acquisition, 46
    of body parts, 70
    categorizing, 44, 69
    practicing, 48, 49
    reviewing, 22, 47, 70
voicing criticism, 59
words and music, making associations
    of, 37
writing
    dialogues, 64
    newspaper headlines, 78
    sentences, 60
    creative, 19, 34
    practicing, 22

SUGGESTED LEVELS

all levels, 22, 26, 36
elementary, 25, 71
elementary to intermediate, 60, 69
low intermediate, 38
low intermediate and above, 9, 44, 46
intermediate, 13, 14, 16, 18, 19, 20, 21,
    23, 32, 37, 52, 59, 64, 70, 72, 79
intermediate and above, 5, 6, 7, 8, 12,
    24, 28, 29, 34, 40, 41, 42, 43, 54, 55,
    58, 75
high intermediate, 66, 67
high intermediate to advanced, 2, 10,
    31, 45, 47, 62, 68, 78
variable, 48, 49, 52, 56